CW00850467

THE *Five Suns* of *Amatory*

MAXWELL DAVIS

ISBN: 978-1-09835-612-5 Print
ISBN: 978-1-09835-613-2 eBook

CONTENTS

THE DECLARATION OF

Acknowledgements

- First and foremost, giving all glory and honor to my Lord and Savior for His showers of blessing, continuing life and love experiences and the very hidden talent of Poetic Writing to complete the book successfully.

- To my loving Family: My Mother, The always admired and highly respected Reverend (*Cherry Blossom*). To my loving Sister, the Strong (*Magnet*) and best older Sister, Author, Scholar, and Friend a little brother could have in his life. In loving memory of my Step Father, Lt. Frank Woods, (*The Armed Force*) of the family. In loving memory of my Father, Stephen Davis, who was an Avid Reader (Financial Crimes was the flavor), a real (*Knicks*) fan and will remain as the real OG of Brooklyn, NY. To my loving Grandparents, thank you for always being there. Last, but not least, my cousin Jordan Davis, the best "little brother" I never had.

- To all my friends, thank you for your continued support and ears when listening to the drafts of these "Muzik-Ties".

- To all the future Artists, Poets, Hopeless Romantics, Inspiring Storytellers, Musicians (critics and listeners), Dreamers turned Achievers, Future collaborators and new couples... Tell your story and live your Truth.

- Finally, To Number 88. *"We may not have as much time together as we would've wanted but the sweet moments we did will always remain."*

THE DECLARATION OF

Disclaimer

The Five Suns of Amatory was written to provoke
a conversation about the conduct and dynamics of
contemporary relationships, gender roles and issues of love.

am·a·to·ry

Amatory

adj.

Of, relating to, or expressive of love, especially romantic love

I wrote this all for you as my actions of
Infatuation.
I wrote this all for you as my actions of
Seduction.
I wrote this all for you as my actions of
Dalliance.
I wrote this all for you as my actions of
Devotion.
I wrote this all for you as my actions for your…
Decision.

THE FIRST DECLARATION OF DEDICATION:

The Infatuation of Satin and Soul

I'm often known to speaking in codes,

Mixing the truth and some fantasies

Down this life and of bumpy roads

Moments where I did and didn't blow it

At the end of all these testimonies

Hoping that you will see through it

It's time to tell you the First part of the truth...

Welcome to The Five Suns of Amatory:

The Infatuation of Satin and Soul

#1 Heaven and Reality (Part One)

The Declaration of Introduction:
One day as I was walking down the street.
The rhythm of the city was on the beat
The people on their phone talking and texting
The dogs in the main park barking and stretching
My city's always moving, never ever stopping
This perfect muse
I cannot lose
Then I saw someone amazing. Yes. You.
This story I swear it's (almost) true
(She's) Ready, (I'm) Set, (Let's) Go!

Part One:
From the coffee shop she turns from the corner
Looking across the street, I had to get to know her
With an angelic glow, she looked like a winner
Take her out on a date, even pay for dinner
To me, she could be my Soul Simmer.
Was blind, but now I can see
Between you and me
She was no longer my fantasy
From her, I saw Heaven and Reality.

Part Two:
Beauty so blinding (I'll bet)
Looking like a runway star
Not worth me dying (Not Yet)
Almost got struck by a subway car.

11

This girl I want to stalk,
Star-struck by the way she walks
As we walked on opposite side
My feelings I cannot hide
From the eyes that cannot stray,
This girl my life I would lay
My word, God does not play
Way to go London Star,
Almost got hit by another subway car.

Part Three:
People tell me that women will be the death of me
To some extent I must (somewhat) agree
My love life is as true as any testimony
Written up like a non-fiction story.
She could be my friend, lover, homie.
She could ride out of any weather so stormy.
Washing and taking away all my pain.
Never lost her soul, so even the world she would gain.
Sensing the celestial energy, she's so spiritual
Like a sold out musical,
Her voice (one could imagine) would be so lyrical
Soothing to the ear, crystal clear
She brought me joys of tears.

Part Four:

As the stars go, she was among the celebrities

In my head that's full of fantasies

These are my Deceptive Art of Storytelling memories.

In the hustle and bustle of the city

She's the definition of Heaven and Reality.

No card, no flowers, or handwritten letter.

I wish I knew her better

Like cursive, she's so fine

Like life, I'm running out of time

In my mind, she can never be irrelevant

As I now fight for my life from the car accident.

#2 Love vs. Lust: A Battlefield

The Declaration of Introduction:
All these other girls can't give me the clear view
You're the hottest girl in my rearview
I just can't stop thinking about you
So stressed out, I can't even unwind
Cause you got me twisted in my mind
Going back and forth of my feelings for you.
Because you got me rolling around like a wheel
When I should be having nerves with Steel
I'm bombarded with this minefield
Between love and lust,
Cause I'm fighting for you in this emotional battlefield.
(She's) Ready, (I'm) Set, (Let's) Go!

Part One:
Love
The hardest feeling
You got my heart really tingling
You got me so messed up when looking at her
And now my feet are approaching her.
She only sees me as a friend.
But in the end, I want her as my girlfriend
Liking you from today or tomorrow
Battling feelings like a sword fight against Sparrow.
Fantasy flirting with you in my head for hours
Then, (in reality) I'm buying you flowers
Putting my heart in the reserves
Everything in life she truly deserves

I want to be the man in the right way
To be with her every day.
My heart is playing the roundabout
Love, please don't count me out.

Part Two:

Lust
You got me in full control
That fiery burning feeling in my soul
This is how this part will begin
Choosing this deadly sin.
How can you blind me like this?
You got me caught up in a twist.
The sexual feelings overpowering
From your simple wave of a sensual touch
I'm trying to fight off this wave of a rush
The burning feeling in my body
This lust is in a form of a lady
I don't want her to be with Somebody.
I don't want her to be with Anybody.
But me. Yeah. Seriously.
This infatuation feeling is like a game
This lust has gotten to me like a moth to a flame
This fire got me uplifting
Walked past me, you got me drifting
Got me singing on some old school Sexual Healing
Into a scenic world of this love vs. lust tour
Now it's time to fight this world on this war.

Part Three:

The Battlefield

The bombs are flying down

Laying down

My life

The heart is so torn

I'm sick of playing hard

I can't fight this feeling anymore

Lust is a burning scorn

Love's the only one that gets the burn

I want you in the way of the lust

But love wants me to get you in trust.

Nerves pounding my heart down like a countdown

On these pages, all I can do is write down…

On the subjects of love and lust

Because I'm fighting for you in this emotional battlefield

And yes, I admit I'm afraid if I lose you

And I go to God to repent

Agreeing with Jordin Sparks for the moment

Tell me how am I supposed to breathe with no air?

Because life without you is unfair.

To all women I will never objectify

I'll tell the truth and testify.

I'm bombarded with this minefield

Between love and lust,

Cause I'm fighting for you in this emotional battlefield.

#3 The Break-Up Testimony (Part One): Dear John

The Declaration of Introduction:
Let's start off with the truth. Yes. After not having a relationship and getting rejected from girls or just not having the heart to ask a popular girl out in fear of rejection, I decided to plan an idea that my heart wouldn't be hurt anymore. Friends with Benefits. New to the concept, but who cared so long as I had someone. Selfish concept? Not even close. Yes. I started off with a friend with benefits with you. Yes. I knew good and damn well I should have stopped it all when you started to have feelings for me and I felt pressured to cave into that concept, but ultimately, I stayed with you for it. Yes, I was so happy after that we were together, even thought that was the wrong way of getting a relationship. Then we had so many problems that I also wanted to end it, but I didn't because you loved me. But you know what? Enough is enough! I cannot stand you anymore for what you did. I wrote you a Dear John Letter to express my closing feelings for you.

(She's) Finished, (I'm) Finished, (Let's) Go!

Part One:
This is my Dear John Letter to you.
This is the end… of you and me.
I cannot live in this world of lies and sorrow.
You are not the girl I fell in love with anymore.
Things between us have changed but only for the worse.
Now I'm starting to believe that you are not a blessing, but a curse.

Part Two:

It is true that we have talked about our problems and other things, but overall, it didn't do anything but ignite the wildfire of more fights and arguments.

All I hear now is false accusation about the things I did and your list of charges against me:

Looking at other girls, talking to girls and not showing you much respect. *(Wait a minute...)*

Not spending enough time with you and not coming through. *(What?)*

The shit that drove me insane was your lack of trust in me. *(What the hell?)*

You hold onto the past mistakes that I did and like a child, I have to conform into someone that I never want to be.

I am not a perfect man and I know you don't expect me to be that perfect one, but I'll be damned if you think that I will stay and keep being drained from the constant arguments between you and I.

There are two sides to every story and I have on multiple counts heard your side and now I am through!

It's OVER! I want you out of my life! I want you out of my life and never return!

I have no reason to stay with you and I am no longer willing to fight for you.

I can't keep promising you the world if only you want to destroy it and only bring much pain for you and me.

You cold hearted treacherous snake of misfortunes and disappointment. Go back to where you once slithered out of the depths of hell you wicked Snake!

Part Three:

I know that last part was harsh, and I am sorry.

How can you even stand to be with me?

After all that I have done to you?

What you have done to me?

This isn't me at all.

The world I once saw, full of color and hope, now an ice box feeling.

So cold and so dark like a shallow grave of the dead.

You took away my warmth and happiness when you stopped trusting me

I have to find someone new to get it back while you do the same.

I'll just stop now and say farewell my love. It was fun while it lasted.

Against my better judgement, I will permit your say in this story.

Our Final Conversation:

Girl: Now wait one God damn minute here! This is not how this Testimony will end! With you coming out as the victim in this!

Mr. Amatory: Sigh. What are you still doing here? I have said that I wanted to say. I am finished.

Girl: Well, I am not. Do you really think that you can run this part of the moment between us? Do you really think you can play victim here? Do you think that you can say your part without them hearing my part?

Mr. Amatory: That's the whole point. I don't want to hear your part anymore with your clingy ass self! I felt so God damn suffocated by you. Worst part? You did that intentionally! This was your plan and you admitted it to me! I didn't want to make you sad anymore. I have seen enough of your tears so I died. I died in the relationship for you to have some kind of happiness between us.

Girl: Like you said, there are two sides to every story, and you will hear my side. After this, we never have to see each other again.

Mr. Amatory: Fine then. Explain. I don't have much time (and neither would anyone else). Please sit down.

(The two characters sit across each other in red executive chairs as a spotlight came down on them.)

Girl: Listen to me. You never reassured me that you only had eyes for me, you flirted with other girls, when I would tell you a story you interrupted me to start another conversation with somebody else and then when you were done that's when you remembered me, you didn't respect me, sure my body but never me. I guess the clingy started when you wanted to hide our relationship and I guess deep down it was my way of sort of staking a claim or something, but it all backfired on me.

Mr. Amatory: You damn right it did. I'm sorry that I didn't do it earlier, but we both know why and no one else needs to know more. I meant no disrespect at all. I never flirted with a girl that was not you. I gave compliments that were meaningless. At the end of the day, my heart was still going to you and only you.

Girl: And I never knew that. You hardly opened up to me. You never voiced how you were feeling until I had to force it out of you. You waited until we had an argument to say anything that was bothering you.

Mr. Amatory: I didn't wait until we had an argument to say anything that was bothering me. I had no fucking choice because you created the arguments with your passive responses and moods. You told me once that you only argued with me to get me to open up and I deeply resented you for that. I never been wanted to argue or tell you anything until I wanted to tell you when I felt like it.

Girl: Which was close to never or when I had to force it out of you. I felt it was the only way for you to talk openly and honestly to me about anything. I had no other choice or any other idea as to how to just get you to talk to me.

22

Mr. Amatory: This is getting us nowhere.

Girl: Are you not happy with me anymore?

Mr. Amatory: Relationship wise, yes. I am not happy with you anymore. That is why I broke up with you.

Girl: You really did break my heart. You did. I hope that's what you get after this. For another girl to break your heart. Worst part? You kept this thought in your mind and you weren't man enough to tell me that you were unhappy and was going to dump me in the beginning of the New Year.

Mr. Amatory: Let me tell you *one last time* why I did this and then I'm finished talking to you. From time to time there were times where it was great to be with you, but then when we argue and there is drama, it makes me more distant from us. Another idea is that I didn't get to really know you as my dear friend. I jumped into friends with benefits with you and then a relationship and now as I am away from you, I feel light as a feather caught in a breeze and less bounded by you to escape the drama we always get into.

Girl: I'm done hearing this. You really are a selfish bastard. Remember, I loved you more than you did me. Maybe sexually you did love me, but emotionally, you didn't. Be real about that.

Mr. Amatory says nothing and only give her a look before sighing.

Girl: You're not the man I thought I knew. Just a wasted man with no hope for any woman that you pursue and look where you are now. Such a shame, especially when a boy like you cannot even be a real man. It's over. Piss off your life without me.

#4 Surrender (The Unconditional Love Version)

The Declaration of Introduction:

*"Unconditional love is about accepting your partner as they are, which
includes all the flaws that make them human,
and without expecting them to change to fulfil your
own ideas of how a partner should be."*
~Valentina Tudose, Clinical Hypnotherapist and Trainer

(She's) Ready, (I'm) Set, (Let's) Go!

Part One:

Known for moving too fast for a companion
I've falling in too many canyons
For your heart, still worth standing
Sailing on some Rhythm and Blues
When my heart starts to slow down
Making the right decision to you
Renouncing the world to make you my girl
All your Quirks and your Perks
I'm ready to go down to work
You said I love being your girlfriend
I said, I love being your best friend
I just want you to love me and trust me
Maybe we will still be travelling buddies?
I just want you on my side, I just want you to be my side,
Are you ready to go on this ride?

Chorus:

Listen to me closely like a symphony
See Me as I See You
I love you unconditionally
You are a dream come true
To my eyes, you are such a star
Don't ever change who you are
To these words, just remember
My Unconditional Surrender

Part Two:

Okay, you're imperfect, I'm imperfect
Wait; I'm just scratching the surface
You make mistakes, I make mistakes
But for love's sake…
Flaws and all, I stand with you
You and me against the world
I'll support you in all your dreams
Some passion and some fashion
Ha-ha. I'm running up a theme
That's why you'll always get the cream
My love for you will never shift
On those days you need a lift
I'll shower you with some gifts
Not buying your love; don't drift
Babe, you should already know
I'm not doing this action for show
I'll give you the world with a bow
Cause truthfully, I'm falling for you
Free falling on love and security

Kissing you and becoming my remedy
I'll stand proud and tall as your defender
With you on my mind, I will surrender
When you call me your forever

Chorus:

Listen to me closely like a symphony
See Me as I See You
I love you unconditionally
You are a dream come true
To my eyes, you are such a star
Don't ever change who you are
To these words, just remember
My Unconditional Surrender

Part Three:

On Love, I will pay the bounty
trading my life for yours proudly
Singing this next part loudly
I love you; I want you madly
We only have one life to live
All of you I want desperately
Passionately, badly, and quickly
Asked for your hand; you said gladly
A ring on your finger, let this moment linger
Celebrating you and only you forever
(That's more like it…)
Let me become your favorite singer
(And become your number one hit)

Chorus:

Listen to me closely like a symphony
See Me as I See You
I love you unconditionally
You are a dream come true
To my eyes, you are such a star
Don't ever change who you are
To these words, just remember
My Unconditional Surrender

#5 From Jordans to High Heels

Part One:

Babe,

From your head to your toes

You look so unreal

In this life, you will grow

That's me being real

The way you rock those jean shorts

But look stunning that dress

The way that you rock my boat

Damn right I'm impressed

You can kick back with the homies

Wearing Puma, Jordans, Adias, Nike

I think she likes me; I think she likes me

I took my time to get to know you well

In the right state of mind

Got my heart and my mind in symmetry

Because you are one of a kind!

We rock in matching tracksuits like pros

That's how this story will be told

You got all the guys in the neighborhood

Checking you out in your expensive Jordans

But you are living like everything's Golden

My boys dogging me that you might be the one

You can keep it real with me as we have some fun

I can keep it real with you

Let's move to Part two

Part Two:

From Jordans to High Heels
You got the stylist look
From Jordans to High Heels
You got the fliest look
From the Gucci to Prada
Sexy Lingerie to Nada
Please excuse me Mama
No disrespect on you
But you brought Jimmy Choo
Some Louis, Miu Mui
Even some Red Bottoms too
All on your dime, all on your dime
Girl, can you spare me your time?
From those sexy heels on your feet
You can play both sets of that beat
A lady in the street and a freak in the sheet
Come over in your heels and a trench coat
Wake up next morning to some French Toast
You love that I'm the type of guy
That doesn't have to try flexing
You love that you can come to me
When you cry and not go straight to sexing
You said just take your time to be mine
I love that I can come kick it with you anytime
By you and I can remain true and fine

Part Three:

From Jordans to High Heels
You got the stylist look
From Jordans to High Heels
You got the fliest look
You rock both worlds of shoes
You make my dreams come true
You make me feel like a star
While we go in the Midnight hour
Maybe we can smoke a little over some weed
Maybe we can joke a little if that's all we need
To unwind and spread some Slow Jam
Rotate on some old school music
Rub you down and call it therapeutic
Sex around and still be friends with matching styles
With you as my home girl that I can make you smile
To us hiding our midnight affair from Jordans to High Heels

#6 Intimate After Hours I: Sex on Fire

Part One:

Crimson rose petals and burning sapphire

The thick smoke of passion and desire

From your appetizing taste to your perfect scent

To the sparks when our bodies reconnect.

The Flames growing higher

As Your Kisses feel lighter

The touch is so hot

Let's call it the G-Spot.

As Valuable as Heaven's galore

Entering your pleasure core,

Performance was so good; you'll be saying encore!

As we mix into our deepest fantasy,

All I want is you and your sexy body,

As the room gets hotter,

You and me; it's no bother

Deep rubs to release (sexual) tension

Thrusts is to moans, as sparks is to combustion.

Now I want your full attention

Because when it comes to sex, I have no restriction

Of you cumming

Down like lava flowing

As bright as a firefly, your beauty is showing.

I love your sex that gives me much delight

Go now and ignite the night

And say in the end, that it's all right.

Part Two:

There is no cure, no sleep and no remedy

My feelings for you is in deep jeopardy

Blinded by sex, let the vision be clear

The trail of fire is drawing nearer

To us on the bed

Cheeks turning red

Who cares if we are alive or dead?

As one last kiss draws us closer

We maintain in perfect composure

In this final hour,

As you bloom like a springtime flower

You have all the power

Panting, moaning, and groaning

As we perspire

Drinking, Sexing and cruising

I want to take you higher

You are the truth, the whole truth

Celebrate as we just had Sex on Fire.

#7 Intimate After Hours II: Heavenly Inferno

The Declaration of Introduction:
Escape from this realm and be free
Tonight, you are alone with me
My feelings for you is all I got
So, I'll say it again, I want to hit that spot
Like a target, ready aim fire.
Let me take you higher
Flower trails on the floor,
You're the one I really adore
From the flexibility, so easy to bend
My feelings for you, where would it end?
You say, Quiet on set
As we kiss in the closet
As we're sexing in the Bedroom,
As we're sexing in the bathroom,
No end to this moment.
From the front to the back porch
As you light the wooden torch
Faultless, I would not blame her
The night she unlocks my chamber
Bra and panties set with the red rose
The real inspiration to write this prose
What we do here tonight, anything goes
Let's simply call it, Heavenly Inferno.
(She's) Ready, (I'm) Set, (Let's) Go!

Part One:

Tonight, I need you.

In pure desperation

With you, I have nothing to lose.

I made a dinner reservation

For me and you

Cause tonight we are sexin' for two.

From the savory steak to your sexy sorbet,

You are the perfect gourmet!

On this cherry wood table,

This is no ordinary fable

I'm serving your body like Thanksgiving,

Your aroma is elevating,

Your sex is stimulating

This is only the beginning.

As MJ once said, You Rock my World

Without you, my body is so ice cold

Warm me up right now

Gunning your spot like pow

The best of both Worlds

You are my Midnight Girl

So sweet and full of spice.

Russian roulette style; roll the dice.

Take this chance

At this passion of romance.

Like a sauna, your body is steaming

Sweating down faster than a hot summer's night

Opening you up like a piñata

Playing songs like *Why you Wanna*

Going round after round until mañana.

Part Two:

A woman's worth is so much more than a dollar

Every time you scream and holler

The Scorching Sensual Fire we make, changing in color

As we enter a new hemisphere

Just you and me. Right now. Right here.

We will be alright in the end

That's the beauty of you being a homie, lover, friend.

Take center stage and bow

Let me take you down now.

Give the people what they want and Roar

I applaud you and say you I truly adore.

From the friction touch of my stubble face

To us burning through rubber, this is the case.

By the end of this round

We will burn this whole house down

Let's not try to run and hide

As the embers flying around outside

Part Three:

The sex between us was so lit
Neighbors look at us like misfits.
I'm not the one to blame
They now know your name
As you and I are just a sexy little flame.
Let's trail off into the backyard
Thinking long and hard
You were the perfect blowtorch
From the front to the back porch
In the place that only we know
Bra and panties set with the red rose
The real inspiration to write this prose
What we do here tonight, anything goes
Let's simply call it, Heavenly Inferno.

#8 Intimate After Hours III: Diamond Storm

Part One:
Of our new life; it's the norm
The is the perfect Diamond Storm
Part of the next hemisphere
It's just us now. Right here.
You and me in your room.
Watching a movie between Deep and Bloom.
Playing video games
Laughing and creating nicknames
Singing old school songs in style
I love the way you make me smile.
Between us, we are in the moment
Like Heaven, no sadness or sorrow
No adversary, no opponent
With you, not today or tomorrow.
The start of the storm filled with energy flows
So powerful it shatters all the windows
Lightning strikes around downtown
Time for the countdown:
(Can you Hear it?)
The slow rumble of thunder in the sky?
(Can you Feel it?)
The intense heat in the air?
(Can you Smell it?)
The cracking burning wood on a winter night?
(Do you see what I see?)
The sky swirling from a sapphire dark blue to crimson ruby sky.

The booming thunder of a God as the earth is slowing down in rotation.

The perfect weather; so sensational.

Your voice that takes away the pain.

Diamonds begin to rain

Shining brighter than a lo-star

In this scene of life, be my co-star.

Part Two:

This is the greatest story ever told

The ground is paved with gold

Slippery when we glide

Take off your shoes and let's slide.

Picking up diamonds off the ground

You have a special gift on command

A diamond not consumed by the fire

No graze, no pain, no burn

Handed me the gem and said 'your turn'

Burned my hands, you said 'so much to learn'

Let's walk over to the top of the hill

Overseeing the meteor shower

From the beauty that would kill

Beauty as bright as the Eiffel Tower

This is the eye of the storm

Where the air is nice and warm

Give ear to the storm and listen

I'm such a ruthless Pirate.

You're my perfect Assassin

#9 Intimate After Hours IV: Rainforest

The Declaration of Introduction:
As our Sex Drive is faster than a high-speed chase,
Imagine us in a brand-new place.
The air is cold crisp and breezy
This mist in the air taste so sweet as whisky.
From the tallest trees to the fertile ground
To the tastiest fruit that is heavenly renowned.
The sweetest sensation in the soul
Serve it to you in a dinner bowl.
From my talk of this
This temptation; do not resist.
As we enter this place of the Rainforest.
(She's) Ready, (I'm) Set, (Let's) Go!

Part One:
The days and nights changes like a mood ring
All I want to do is say girl you good… sing
Absorb the good vibes like Eden
Do you get what I'm feeling?
I want to hear you screaming
Be free and unleashed your earthly burden
Your true feelings for a brother?
Don't you even fake.
Let's cleanse each other
In these great lakes.

Embrace from water that will soon turn into mystical fire.

Created from our sexual desire

These flames will not burn thee.

Rather promote happiness. See?

Part Two:

Blinding to the eyes, I barely see

Thick as smoke, temptation is around me

Wrapped your body around me like a snake on a prey

You soon pounce on me with no delay,

Whispered in my ear, you say… "Let's play".

Snuck some fruit from the Forbidden Tree

Mixing sin and whisky; we're floating like a bee.

The first sinful taste of your lips, so sweet and juicy

Body so smooth like a new Bentley

Two lovers in the heat of lust

Pure adrenaline between us

No friction,

No restriction

Just listen…

Combust equal friction plus spark plus motion.

From us hanging out to talking

Hand to hand walking

Warm bodies close in our movement

In the place of pure fun and our amusement.

Part Three:

You got me really thinking

I cannot control this sexual feeling

I taste your sweet waterfall

Sweeter than a shopping spree at the mall

Whenever you want babe, give me a call

I only want you to be truly satisfied

When you cum, my actions are purely justified

The atmosphere is so full of life

As we just stop and cuddle undercover

#10 Her (Final) Advice

The Declaration of Introduction:

I just came back from many trips and traveled the world. I saw so many places and so many people that some would kill to have my lifestyle. I am not boasting, quite frankly I'm being extremely humble about what I have experienced. I get back to my dresser and notice a letter on my dresser with a single rose and my name across it. I knew the signature and the red lipstick to seal it. I knew it was you. I haven't heard from her in over five years. When it came to asking for advice, She was the only girl I knew I could call; day or the night. I could blame time, but this time I was in the wrong for not catching up. I can blame the fame life and other things, but I must be a man and accept the facts. I open the envelope. There were four post cards with three of her pictures attached to them and a letter.

(She's) Ready, (I'm) Set, (Let's) Go!

Part One:

Hey. What's good baby? I know that it has been three years and I know that you haven't been checking up on your girl.
Based on the postcards, you can see that I have also traveled the world.
Do you remember when you...
Asked me for advice like in the old days?
Boy, tell me why are you acting this way?
Why is your heart so cold and has gone astray?
You finally got famous and have changed for the worst.
You truly have changed for the worst.
With your greatest success of your novel of stories...
(Ah. Testimonies.)

When most of them are about you and me homie?

If you can't admit to that part, then that is quite scary.

I know that honestly, without me you feel very lonely.

I was there with you from the very start.

You were the thief that stole my heart.

Was that a crime? I simply say it's not your fault.

Do you remember when you ran to me for advice?

I gave you only the truth and not made up lies.

Now you don't even want to hear me or even listen.

Calling me out and asking why I'm bugging?

When you acting so tough like you mean mugging?

(This ain't you boy.)

Part Two:

From the flashing lights and your candid answers that are so crappy,

Lie to the world, but you can't to me…I can tell that you are unhappy.

Many people in your famous life, including those famous girls,

I can see behind the sunglasses you are so done with this famous world.

Do you remember all the good times we had together?

Before she came along and became your endeavor?

I mean I feel your pain boy, but don't take your fear of denial overshadow
what could be.

I'm your true home girl and you know it.

Why don't you believe me?

I'm not like most girls that comes in your life just for a season.

I want to be with you all year round and explain that I'm your reason.

You fire back in retaliation in saying my accusations are just counterfeit.

My response: You are seriously full of shit.

Yelling and cursing at me saying all girls are the same,

I laugh at that concept and call you insane.

All wanting your fame and all your money.

(I swear, I wasn't trying to be that funny.)

But, is it them that you can even blame?
Boy, she doesn't even want to take your last name.
When the poker chips fall, she would leave you alone to suffer.
Maybe then boy, you will finally get it together.
And I guess in some sense you are right, but that is not me.
But who am I to step into your life anymore?
Still give you advice when you act like you are so grown?
You don't see me like you did before.
I get it now. She is your endeavor that you will cherish forever.
I'm the girl you no longer want to remember.

Part Three:
Word to the wise
I only wanted to give you one final piece of advice:
Never forget who was with you from the very start.
Never forget that I was the thief that stole your heart.
Because I never forgot about you and your accepting loving self.
I guess it truly is the end.
All I can say now is goodbye and farewell Friend

#11 Future Predictions

The Declaration of Introduction
I saw you in my dreams, but it felt like a new day
You rose up from the ashes after you went to slay
Anything and anyone that got in your way
Unapologetic of your justified actions
Becoming that woman that's successful, professional and incredible
Being a role model, who can buy her own bottles, rides on full throttle
Chasing your dreams, creating scenes and your record being clean
So bold with your achievements, let them admire you…
Hands down my dear, you deserve line of respect
Writing the next two parts, you better come correct
(She's) Ready to listen, (I'm) Set, (Let's) Go!

Part One:
Stamping everything we ever did with authenticity
We start off on some flirtation with no limitation
Maybe even think that this moment is synchronicity
Your name, my name, neither playing any games
Can we start off as you and me being just homies?
We started off being cool when she labeled you as a fool
Simple infatuation without appreciation?
The world deemed you as a bad distraction
Down to my last breath, I will dispute that last line
Who is she to say with her misdirection?
They look at you as the one that will steal my time
Wild accusations call for full annihilation
They don't know of the things that you do
They don't know of the things that you do

I love the way you make me feel
You take all my words seriously
I love the way you make the deal
You and me, we can keep it real
I mean that truly and honestly
You are the only woman that I will drop the L word
Yep. The L word.
Listen up.

Part Two:
You play so coy and innocent unlocking my desires
You know all my wildest desires under the fire
Secrets that only you will understand without judgement
I lust for your heart and approval without any punishment
Your feeling on me as we listen to some R&B Singers
Mixing feelings and drinking as the night lingers
Three kisses on your neck and you are smiling
Two kisses on your lips and we are drinking
Sex on the mind as my hands goes climbing
Up your dress as you have me Against the Wall
Imaging pleasing you as your lacy panties fall
I'm deep in your head so let's move to your bed
All the sexual positions we can do and mesmerize
Unleashing the beast in me with bloodshot eyes
Only you babe, my mind and heart will visualize
When you read the end for your last surprise
My final confession on this Infatuation
That is my only question to your perfection
Will you be satisfied or left out hung to dry?

#12 The Last World Tour (Part I): Paige

The Declaration of Introduction:
Well World, Anything Goes
In my Last World Show.
The Plane is Landing
My fans are screaming.
No idea for what's in store
This is my Last World Tour.
All the other girls could only put a smile on my face
But in Full circle of reality, you were well worth the chase.
Cause you were the one that can slay
Hit pause, rewind, and press play.
(She's) Ready, (I'm) Set, (Let's) Go!

Part One:
World Tour for my best friend
Soul Search for my girlfriend
From my Soul's Out Crowd
To the girls who like to get down.
Swagger like Snoopy
So many Groupies
Groupie Girls are my sincere addiction,
Sex with them are my genuine prescription.
At the end of it all, I just want a girlfriend.
Met this girl at the meet and greet
Her attitude was sarcastic and sweet.
Telling me her name was Paige,
I told her to come backstage
She and I shared the same energy
Wondering to myself, is this destiny?

Games, jokes, and simple lust
We both desire one thing: simple trust.
Of our time together, we exchange life stories
Mine's the same, just call them Testimonies.

Part Two:
Over time we became the best of friends
She was on top of the charts, the perfect trend.
Sunday-Friday Hotel Parties of a Rock Star
Partying, Dancing, Gaming to the music beat
Drinking, Smashing, Sexing in the Rock Suite
Just living the life, no regret,
So glad she and I just met.
As she's going up town
I'm going downtown
As she sings the perfect sound.
We hit the club, we get to the dance floor
We got close and she said she wanted more.
Step by step of the tempo
First class girl gets the memo.
Body so good, call her Master Thriller
Slaying the dance floor, she's a Master Killer
We both tipsy
Off the drinks of martini
First kiss and it was minty.
She dances like a drunken stripper
Grab the body and only want to strip her.
In the dark club cave, she's the only one who shines
Spying other girls, she pulls me in and says, 'You're mine!'

Part Three:

Telling jokes that were so outdated,

Drinking, Sexing, blowing till we got faded.

She said to Start it off slow

As she loves her Kisses Down Low.

We are running up the score like an arcade

Sex was sweeter than lemonade

Drunken off that cheeky wine

My World Tour is running out of time.

All I want is a girl who will love me and listen

She said that she wants me and a few kisses.

Love, Sex, Money. No Issues.

Seven Days Later, damn give her a tissue.

My World Tour was coming to an end,

I'm about to lose my sex friend.

All I can say in the end of the Tour,

I had no idea of what was in store

Between me and the World Stage

This girl, her name was Paige

Only seeing her as a fantasy

Like my other Story

She's now my Heaven and Reality

But I'm not leaving her without a fight.

No. Not Tonight.

Paige, I'm coming for you

As I close Part one and write Part two.

#13 R&B Crushes

The Declaration of Introduction:
Women are as beautiful as a song.
If loving isn't right, then call me wrong.
You plus me, its simple logic,
Like gossip, our love is the hot topic.
Without you, it's like a bullet without a pistol,
But without you, I won't shatter like a piece of Crystal.
Love is long and a wondrous lesson,
Many women in this poem had the best impression.
To these women, both young & old, they gave me the case of the blushes
Like a song, these are my R&B crushes.
(She's) Ready, (I'm) Set, (Let's) Go!

Part One:
From her past of playing the board game Sorry
She grew up from her House Party
Drunken off the Bacardi
Took her out and drove her around my Maserati
Sex appeal babe look at your body!
She got to me so quick
But she's so sexy and slick
All the guys went to her and only mack
Pure lines and feelings for her they really lack.
Really, she is a perfect 90's throwback.
Like a hot summer's day, she's walking down the street
Every time she walked passed me; she made this heartbeat.
White tank top, light blue jeans
She's sweeter than a jellybean

London Fog that is such a blur
Head over heels, I've Fallen for her.
Her sex appeal matches her video.
My Love is like... Wo
80 in a 30-style babe,
(She's) Ready, (I'm) Set, (Let's) Go.
Mysterious as a simple black thong.
Slow jams is the name of this song.
Don't cost a thing, I can't buy ya
Knock out you are girl, hi-ya!

Part Two:
This first girl I knew in the past
I was young and my feelings were moving fast.
Role of a girlfriend I wanted her to cast.
Back in the day, we were best friends
Showing me a picture from way back
Simply saying: This is me... then.
Like a young Jenny from the Block.
To her sexy attitude to her twisting hair-locks
Straight, curly, twisted, Afro.
Appealing type of girl from her head to her toes
Rocking the cut-out shorts that showed some Booty
Had to stare, but she is such a cutie when she produced her movie
Like LL Cool J, I want her to come around my way,
We can Get Right before the night
Over the Floor shining moon light
As soft as the fall breeze, my heart for her will not sway
Without her, it's not an option I'm willing to pay
Don't want to be riding solo
Be with me tonight, don't leave just stay.
You Only Live One Life

Part Three:

This next girl I knew was so chill
When I was with her, she could make time stand still.
I got the Keys to her Diary,
Your secrets are safe with me.
Trust and believe me.
Even after writing her hits on her Typewriter.
She rose like a Phoenix singing This Girl is on Fire
She was the perfect melody
Angel in mirage so heavenly
Let's toast up your success over cheese and wine
All we have in this world is time.
I want you to come with me
Open and be free
Our love is Unbreakable (Steady)
Trust me and say the Un-Thinkable (I'm Ready).

Part Four:

My dream wedding would be on the beach with black sand
Walking barefoot side by side holding hands
Just stating facts.
Before we get to that,
On some 90's Brandy,
I Wanna Be Down with you
Let the world Talk About Our Love
In the Full Moon.
Skin so dark like Hennessy
Lips so sweet as Whisky
Drunken off her attention
I need your affection.
Your voice is a song, it's poetry
Please Say Yes like Floetry.

My friends and family ask me one question:

Who is She 2 U?

I tell them. My Boo.

Damn, I don't deserve you.

I don't just want you,

I need you.

I only want to love you.

Show yourself off and flaunt

You can have whatever you want

You are crazy and I'm insane

Be my life, my wife and take my last name.

Conclusion:

Life is a game

I'm tired of playing.

Sweet honeycomb.

But I'm living in such a Cole World...

"Too young to bring Aliyah home".

Now, I'm all alone.

Age Ain't a Number

Now I must get back up and Try Again.

Damn. Bummer.

Love is a lesson,

Many women in my life had the best impression.

All these women in my past made me blush

But it's just a story of my R&B Crushes.

#14 (The) Verdict of Devastation (Crystalize Scripted Interlude)

The Crystalized Scripted Interlude:
So many women in my life I will truly front
Because you're the only girl I truly want.
But I can't have you because of time
I wanted you to be mine.
Don't want to cross that line,
The world is moving too fast for me
You don't want to remember the past of you and me.
Is it worth me going through this pain?
Is it worth me going insane?
Writing about you.
                    (Do you even care?)
Drinking about you.
                    (With or without some swears?)
Thinking about you.
                    (Do you even care?)
Are you even there?
                    My heart holding on to this.

Mr. Amatory: Sara, you will be my deciding fate in this corrupted world as a good man is sent away for twenty years. Before I am taken away, I want you to hear everything I have felt about you. My love for you. My true love for you. I have nothing else in my life anymore. Friends gone, family left, and my adversary has broken me down. I have lost. But please. I need your answer on this final testimony.

He looks down as she wipes Mr. Amatory's tears away.

Sara: I don't understand why you still would call for me after all this time, but since you have nothing anymore, I might as well hear you out one last time. What is your final testimony to me?

#15 Crystalize

The (Back) Declaration of Introduction:
Previously on #14....

(She's) Reading, (I'm) Truth Telling, (Let's) Go.

Part One:
So many girls and I was going insane
Then I met you and I never was the same
I remember you, you shining gem
You were the Crème de la Crème
As kids, we were the best of friends
From way back when
Then Time came in and created a wedge
Going crazy like Hammy, Over the Hedge.
Without you in my life, I'm going over the edge
I'm living to this mirage
(When drinking about you)
I'm driven to this façade
(When writing about you)
Heart's fixing on this sabotage
(When thinking about you)
Telling family and my friend
You and I will one day be wed.
Time's moving so fast
Guess my mind's living in the past
Only remembering the girl as my best friend
From way back when.

Chorus:

You and me I can only visualize

Your beauty makes me paralyzed

Pieces of my heart is starting to Crystalize

As I start to realize

I want you to be mine

But can't because of time

You moved on so fast from me

You don't want to remember the past of you and me.

The memories of us you don't want to cherish it

So as cold as death, I'll perish with it.

But is the pain of you

Really worth

The Hurt?

Part Two:

As we're growing older

In this imperfect world

In the past I should have told her

She's my perfect girl

My love for you is a boomerang

Throwing hate on you in one direction

Then wanting you back in the same direction

I know this line will be a cliché

But I can't stop thinking about you

Almost every day.

I know that girl in my past world

Will not be the same in this fast world.

As I'm screaming to the Heavens above

I'm begging Cupid to let me be the one for you.

To allow me to shower you with my eternal love

Unlock her heart and burn her with my key

As she says she doesn't remember anything about me
As she now looks at me like a dangerous man.
When I know that I am a generous man.
As I'm going insane,
Adding salt to my pain
Now you are with another guy
Nope. Nope. I will not believe that lie
Now Heaven hear the roar of my cry.

Chorus:
You and me I can only visualize
Your beauty makes me paralyze
Pieces of my heart is starting to Crystalize
As I start to realize
I want you to be mine
But can't because of time
You moved on so fast from me
You don't want to remember the past of you and me.
The memories of us you don't want to cherish it
So as cold as death, I'll perish with it.
But is the pain of you
Really worth
The Hurt?

Part Three:
Writing about you in stories and letters,
I feel a bit better.
I want to be the one to take care of her.
It's such a damn shame
That Time and love are making me play this game
So many times, the mind said "forget her and move on"
So many times, the heart said, "That's just wrong!"

Never felt like this before
Against the mind and heart, it's a bloody war
Knock me out the park like Ruth
Time for me to accept the truth
I'll take this shock like a taser
It's no longer worth to chase her
I'll take this pencil and erase her
If that be the case.
Even through my heart's already crowned you first place.

Chorus:
You and me I can only visualize
Your beauty makes me paralyze
Pieces of my heart is starting to Crystalize
As I start to realize
I want you to be mine
But can't because of time
You moved on so fast from me
You don't want to remember the past of you and me.
The memories of us you don't want to cherish it
So as cold as death, I'll perish with it.
But is the pain of you
Really worth
The Hurt?

#16 Heaven and Reality (Part II): Intoxicating Coma

The Declaration of Introduction:
From your intoxicating aroma,
I'm so deep into my coma.
My life is on the line from the car accident
How low can I go?
Well Honestly,
I really can go that low.
Like taking the perfect ecstasy
You got my head soaring like a Sonic Wave
(Swirling around like rings of color!)
You got my head banging like a Sonic Rave
(Come dance with a Brother!)
In the hustle and bustle of this faultless city,
You seem so unreal with that faultless body
She's the definition of Heaven and Reality.
But this time around,
I'm trying to understand
Where we stand in this world.
Listen up girl.
(I'm) Ready, (She's) Set, (Let's) Go!

Part One:
First thing you hear is the heartbeat of the city
The fast cars, the fast bikes, the fast nights in the streets
The authentic rhythm of the city was on beat
Next thing you see is the Street lights, feeling the Street music and the
women of the city
All these other players are chasing the scene

I pull up and I frame the scene
She pulls up and she makes the scene
Tonight is your night
Cause it's all about you.
Got my heart racing like Audi
Got my mind thinking like you somebody
You got me so twisted
From your intoxicating aroma,
I'm so deep into my coma.
But your presence is so gifted
Legendary Style let's Get Lifted!

Part Two:
Time to get my flirt on,
When I don't even know your name
But that's just the turn on,
When you got me playing mind games
She told me that I need to find some game
Only looking at your Instagram
All I can say is damn.
I've made a decision
You are the definition
Of a smoky sexy vision.
Listen.
I want you
In a lustful way
You want me
In a trustful way.
Like a poet to a sonnet
I'm just being honest.
So, Say it's alright babe
Let's just have sex tonight babe.

I bet you do well in bed
Cause you got my head rising from the dead.
Sorry. I don't mean no disrespect
But you're the girl I really want to get
I'll be the man that you will never forget
Don't pass me by
Stay with me tonight
Don't say goodbye
We can leave this bar and I'll pay the fare
Take off your bra as you slowly come out of your sexy underwear.
We can play some Musiq and let me Takeyouthere.

Part Three:
Taking Molly, we're both losing conscious
She's got me swimming in her conscious
Kissing, grinding, flying, running.
Between us, we're simply dying and surviving.
Leaving our state of mind to see anew
Time for this drug to show the real me and you.
Against earth's time, it's half past seven
Outer Space settings, we're half past heaven
In a place of paradise,
Where we can roll the Vegas Dice
The outcome is so nice
Get into the car and let's getaway
We're racing and speeding down the speedway
On the Rainbow road of wonder and galore
So much of you tonight, I truly adore
You make sexing so easy
Almost like magic
You take this loving so easy
As we're sexing in the attic,

Contemplating on a high mind,

We're surfing on the sea of calmness,

But against this high mind,

We're dealing with the enemies of our inner darkness.

We're running out of time.

Like love it's a hell of a puzzle game

Like life, it's a hell of a hustle game

Staying alive against the chase of this white rush

When my heart's mixing love and sex and calls you the right crush.

As I'm just stating facts

Sugar, spice, everything nice, it's so beautifully insane

Sexing you twice, but you still gracefully came

Again, just stating the facts

I'll continue this bliss while cuddling you now.

Part Four:

In the hustle and bustle of this faultless city,

Be the real girl in this aroma fantasy

You seem so unreal with that faultless body

She's the definition of Heaven and Reality.

From your intoxicating aroma,

I'm so deep into my coma.

My Life's on the line from the car accident

How low can I go?

As our high is coming down,

I really can go that low.

I want you to stay around

One last kiss as if our world is crumbling down.

I would renounce my life for you.

So please don't take me from this scheme

This Infatuation Fight is not over. Not yet.

So please don't wake me from this dream

Because we haven't officially met.

#17 Caribbean Skin (Part One)

Part One:
Before you put me to sleep,
Touch me with your Caribbean skin.
Before we go in too deep,
Let's go in for a Caribbean swim
You're so therapeutic
Like a brand-new music
(Say it with me babe.)
You're so therapeutic
Like a brand-new music.
All you ever do is give me the best massages
God, you're the best and ever so flawless.
In this world,
Babe girl.
Teach me how to love,
Like a superintendent
I'll put you above the ranks
Like a Lieutenant
Miss Independent,
The way that you handle yourself,
You can never go left
In my heart, you are so right
And my mind says that it's alright.
The world can be so wrong
Like the Brexit against the pound
But you are the star of this song
That's why you'll stay around.

Part Two:

As we are driving through the heart of the city
Say from time to time that you miss me.
My heart is beating faster than a Sonic Boom,
My heart is beating faster than a Chronic Boom.
You got me speeding like we going 101
Tokyo drifting, we're going to have some fun.
Babe girl,
You're the only one that I want in this world
You want me for the trust
I want you for the lust.
Damn. What a bust.
                    (Such a hard decision. Shit. No. Wait. Listen.)
Right hand on the Bible code,
Love is a bitter game, survival mode
My heart and mind are in rival mode
You simply wrecking these ladies in the end
So, they don't mess with me in the end.

Part Three:

This is my best reward for you
Strip your clothes off for me
This is the sex reward for two,
Let me take you down slowly
Giving it to you all night like I'm on Viagra
I'm falling in your waters like I'm in Niagara.
Swimming deeper into your laps,
Opening your inner flaps
With my teasing tongue
Doing this on repeat, repeat, repeat
Not missing this beat, beat, beat
With me, you'll never ever get bored.

When it comes to me, you can have it all,

Whenever you want me babe, just give me a call.

I'll make you sincerely believe

If you take a chance with me

I'm the Master of Romance babe.

Why postpone this moment?

Let me just dance with her.

Let's play out this moment.

My sign is a Cancer

You in my life is the answer

Her sign is a Scorpio

As you ride me like a Rodeo

Take this chance with me on this flow,

Take the wheel and let's go.

#18 The Last World Tour (Part II): World Tour Revolution

The Declaration of Introduction:

Ladies and Gentlemen!

Thank you, thank you for coming out of the World Tour Revolution

Let me break down a quick introduction.

My Art of Storytelling skills are pure gold

Telling my stories all around the world

True Stories

Still looking for the one to love me. For me.

Expressing myself in this Last World Tour

I got the people behind me

(I got the people behind me)

I got the people behind me

(I got the people behind me)

I got that groupie love on the side

Love, Sex, Money, we've got nowhere to hide

We know how to ride and spend in style

I can take them higher and higher

They all can shine like the stage lights

But really, I want to be with my home-girl Paige tonight.

But just one more girl tonight and everything will be alright.

This girl in the front row

Like a magical illusion

You got that sexy spark and glow

Come up on stage and take this key

By the end of the show, you will set me free.

Time now to rock out this Soul'd Out Show

(She's) Ready, (I'm) Set, (Let's) Go!

Part One:

She got my mind spinning like an old track

Feeling Old school, let's spin that back

She got my mind playing on a SONOS speaker

New school music, she's like a bonus feature.

This girl in the front row I must now engage

I don't want to waste any time

I told her to come up the stage

As I told the band to play the baseline

I told her I'm a Master of Romance

She said too early to tell

Hear my words and be under my trance

I got her under my spell.

So maybe we can do a little Sumthin' Sumthin' like Maxwell.

All jokes aside, all I'm asking is a fighting chance.

I want a girl who's pure in trust

She's got her head in pure wanderlust

Contemplating like a tourist,

She knows I'm the type of guy who can have all of this

She doesn't want a guy who only hit and diss

She wants a guy that can give her the bliss

Excuse my cockiness,

But I can be that guy for you

Yeah, yeah, babe. My word is true.

I'll have your name bigger than Notorious

I'll have your name bigger than Fabulous

Fergie's agreeing with me calling you Glamorous

As the people cheering you on like an audience

In secrecy, I want to see you in your naughtiness.

Part Two:

As we get better with age with your hands in mine,

Let's ride this stage out like the Sands of Time.

Since we ain't private yet

Fly out with me in my private jet

Come up on my stage

Show the world your talent

Live with me in the moment

As we travel over time,

I've been working overtime

Traveling city to city

Off that Sapphire Wine

Going from party to party

You're the life of it.

I want you on my World Tour for the hell of it

Cause without you, This Tour would be irreverent.

Part Three:

As we danced in the nightclub

She was glowing like a light bulb

Body so fit like she does P-90X

Shining like a watch called Rolex

Dancing, drinking, spinning

She's all up in a twirl

She believes she's in her own little world

We can go all night in this life of the party

We can go all night in this life of the party

But Honestly…

I don't want to play any games with you

Take all my words seriously.
You got me thinking of you in sexual fantasies
Be more flexible and take a chance with me.
I'm cool like the midnight ocean breeze
You must come and chill with me.
Make you satisfied until you say qui qui
From London, New York, and even France
I'll take you on so many shopping sprees
Money shower babe, let's dance
By the way girl, I'm a Master of Romance.

Part Four:
When it comes to you texting me, (I'll be around)
When it comes to you sexting me, (you'll win that round)
From the way you make that sound
You got my head up in your cloud
Now clear the room and let me see you.
The real you.
You the type of girl like Sam Puckett
Rebelling against the rules we say fuck it.
Attitude All Grown Up like Susie Carmichael
You got the keys to my motorcycle
You had it all along now don't you know?
You had it all along since the intro.

Part Five:

As we ride out slowly into the night

Ride out with me on this motorcycle beat

Ride out with me and feel this heat

Riding 105 on the 95', we gonna take flight

Behind us, I got the city light

I want you for one night

Because you are the girl that's a rare find

Then in the morning have you until the end of time.

You can have it all without problems or illusion.

You forever changed me babe like the theory of evolution

You in my life is the perfect solution

All because you came to my Last World Tour Revolution.

#19 Type of Guy (Cliché)

The Declaration of Introduction:

We can start out as friends

(So innocently)

Then maybe wanting each other as more than friends

(So Honestly)

To all those other guys you dated in the past

Bury them alive.

They're just a living stereotype.

How can you say that you know me?

Like a damn stereotype?

Don't act like Renee in *The Game*

And say, "[I am] such a cliché" (in this game).

Don't listen to those who hate me

I want you to be that girl to date me.

Ladies, Ladies, Ladies. Please…

How about you let me show you if you were with me?

I can be that type of guy who is not just a fantasy.

But that type of guy who is a reality.

Boyfriend Material.

For real.

Just listen.

(She's) Ready, (I'm) Set, (Let's) Go!

Part One:

Living my life as a single man.

Looking for a woman wasn't in my plans

Damn.

Running around with the women with the mini skirts

Only flirting to get them out of their mini-skirts.

One and done.

Just having some fun.

Sounds selfish (as a man?)

That's the cards I was dealt (as a man.)

So many girls in this city

But then I saw you and said damn

She's so pretty.

I have to be her man.

She said she's heard all of them lines

Sweet lady, I just want a moment of your time

Cause you're worth much more than just a dime

I just want to get to know you better

Before writing you a love letter.

Let me be the one who will lift you

Shower with the finest gifts of you.

Victoria, Tiffany, just to name a few

I'll make your dreams come true!

See, I'm the type that will elevate you

See, I'm the type that will celebrate you

Driving cars so fly on the ride

As we drive past all your ex's

They're still trying to be flexing

Let's start off by saying bye-bye.

Part Two:

Acting like a little kid, I'm a bit shy
Telling you I want to be your guy
You are the girl who glows like fire
You are the girl that I truly desire
Honest girl, I'm not a liar.
I'll write about you like poetry
Write you as my main storyline,
Call you bless like holy wine.
Those other guys can only give you keys of remorse
I'm the type of guy will give you the key to the Porsche
I'll give you all my time and attention
If you can catch my signs and affection.
Giving you compliments from the start
Because in the end, I'm trying to win your heart
Giving you photo colleges
All about you and your beauty
Giving you seven total massages
When you feel a bit moody.
Washing away all your pain
As I'm showering love on you like rain.
As we are all alone, we should just be still
(As we have so much time to kill)
Or we can Netflix and Chill.

Part Three:

At the sight of an honest romance,

Babe, give me an honest chance

Take my word and understand

If you give me your hand,

I'll give you the best plan.

Me. As your best man.

Someone who will hold you close

Someone who will love you the most.

That man who wants you for your heart and soul (For real)

That man who will fight for you and take control (For real)

That man who will make you laugh, smile, and even sing,

Even buy you that perfect diamond wedding ring.

Until then,

Don't let time go by in your life

Say I'm that type of guy in your life

So that someday I can call you my wife.

This Testimony is not a cliché

I want you forever and a day.

Until the very end of our story

When we pass and enter into Glory.

#20 The (Poetic) Actress (Interlude)

The Declaration of Intro-lude:
As she takes off her dark slip.
She has me by her dark grip,
Damn, what a power dark trip.
As she rolls those Red Vegas Dice,
She learns that every action has a reaction.
(She's the) Lights, (I'm the) Camera, (Let's say) Action
Let's get down to the passion.
As we get close into the darkness
we go deep into her true fitness
From our one-night stand
She's rocking me like a marching band.
She's like a gem that is so hard to find
The Infatuation of sex is on my mind
She's blowing up my phone
That's a perfect distraction
She's can't leave me alone
That's a fatal attraction.
She's got me sipping, whipping, flying
Down my own zone.
She's got me tripping, flipping, dipping
Trying to get her home.
Like heaven, she's so flawless
She only knows the life of an actress
And yet with a snap, she can have all of this.
Like a play, that's been rehearsed,
The roles are in reverse.

I should leave her alone,
But she sends me pictures and blowing up my phone.
"These are a no show, so keep these on the low"
Like a play, that's been rehearsed,
She was born to play this part
Like she did with my heart.
As she rolls the Vegas Dice,
Not once, but twice,
She gets a new story and a role
But something better: A new soul.
Nothing more, nothing less
This is her new story: The Actress.
(She's) Ready, (I'm) Set, (Let's) Go!

#21 (The) Actress (Testimony)

The Declaration of Introduction:
Let me give you the Grand Tour
As I am just but an understudy actor
This girl, God truly has blessed her
But now it's time for me to test her.
Something like a Kit Kat,
I broke her moment in Three Acts
In life, she can have all of this
Because of her title of being an Actress.
(She's) Ready, (I'm) Set, (Let's) Go!

Act One:
You can't leave me alone,
That's a fatal attraction
Blinded by the camera phones
That's a perfect distraction.
Black, White, Hispanic, or Asian
It doesn't even matter
Damn, you all have my full persuasion.
So, tell those others to cut the chatter
She got the whole place shut down
On the dance floor, she knows how to get down
All the guys in the club raise your glass
Because she's as fly as first class.
All the world is but a stage…
So now it's time for the friendly exchange.
I asked her for her name
She said that line was lame

(Damn. What a shame).
As I asked for her number,
Her sex appeal was hot as summer.
Her sarcastic remarks were cold as winter
She couldn't remember.
For me, I only had one last chance
Temptation from this girl I cannot resist.
I asked her for the last dance
She said I'm the girl you are going to persist.
Do this right, I'll give you one chance
Get on the floor, let's dance!

Act Two:
Ladies and Gentlemen, I just came to bear witness
This wonderful life of this pure actress!
She likes petting dogs and drinking Starbucks,
Ladies and gentlemen prepare to be starstruck!
One grind, one wink, one touch,
She got me blushing
Moved in for a kiss, she said why we rushing?
I told her she can be my Heaven and Reality,
She laughs… what a Testimony!
Touched my cheek, she said I must be so thirsty,
Touched her side and said yeah, I'm so thirsty.
She likes my game and she want to play
Let's escape and act like a runaway.
We got close and had all night,
One kiss and I got the green light

Intermission:

I said tonight, do you have a man?
She said, tonight you can be my man.
I asked her if she can sing.
She laughs, what does that have to do with anything?
I said just asking her some question,
She said tonight I'm looking for some passion.
I'm your director babe, lights, camera, and action.

Act Three:

She took the condom out of her purse
Performed the sex like it wasn't rehearsed
Those are my favorite verses
All of her I want more and more
She said I'll give you an encore.
Poured her a cup of the Remy
Got her legs up like open sesame
The scene between us was so deep
Bouncing up and down like a 24' jeep
Sex was so good, put us both to sleep.
She was the girl that gave me the bliss
So sad that she was the one who yelled

'dismissed'

#22 If Chivalry is dead, then Why Am I Still Alive?

The Declaration of Introduction:

I know that you think that **all** guys are only ding dongs,

But I'm smoother than most popular love songs.

You got my feeling up like a whirlwind

In the end, I want you as my girlfriend

But you say that all men only act the same

That's the shit that drives me insane

That's the shit that drives me insane.

I tell you that there are still some good men out there

Your simple response: I don't care.

All the men in your life that gave you pain

All the crimes they did to you, I must take the blame.

I'm not playing any games

All I want is for you to take my last name.

You say, 'spare me the lines and the heart break misery.'

I say, hear me out with my story of a man who has chivalry.

(She's) Ready, (I'm) Set, (Let's) Go!

Part One:

Misery always love some company,

You're in need of being with somebody

A man who wants to take care of you

Be there for you

Hell, even love you.

(Despite your daddy issues.)

What do you mean Fuck you?

Son of a bitch woman…

I'm just a man!

For me to love you is the only plan

I'm a man that cannot be duplicated,

So why are you making this so complicated?

In my heart, I will never do any arguing

Let alone disputing

You're making this idea so confusing

Really. Damn those other men

I can be your perfect gentleman

Don't be in the line of fire and misery

I can be your man that has desire and chivalry

Part Two:

Right from the start,

I can be that guy who can win your heart

No lies.

Eyes on the prize

Honor your hope and dreams of all sorts

You in my life is the right answer (of course)

Let me tell you what I can do like a report

Hold the door for you

Call you my muse

Write stories and poems about you

I won't give you any issues

Let me ease you down when you feel like a mess

Tell you that you are the queen in this life called chess

See? I'm such a pro of relieving things including stress

I won't think of you of anything less

Just put me to the test

Really. Damn those other men

I can be your perfect gentleman

Don't be in the line of fire and misery

I can be your man that has desire and chivalry

Part Three:

If chivalry is dead, then why am I still alive for you?

(Tell me)

If chivalry is dead, then why am I making time for you?

(Tell me)

Most men would have given up on you

But like I told you,

I'm not like most dudes.

I want you in my life just for the hell of it

Without you in my life, it would be irrelevant.

These words are forever true

I want to make your dreams forever come true

No one can do me like you could do.

I'll be there to listen to you

Release your disposition of those old dudes

No seriously; (for the last time)

Damn those other men! (for the last time)

With chivalry; (for the last time)

I want to be your perfect gentleman!

#23 T.G.B.S (Thug Gansta Baby Story)

The Declaration of Introduction:
Perfect Anagram
By the way the letters are in a mixture
Perfect Instagram
By the way you show in your pictures
The girl at the top?
Yeah, she's alright with me
Right at the very top
Even if she thinks she can out annoy me.
So please don't find this story on the offense.
Hope this story will not put you in the defense
But this is the only way I can truly express it all
Let this story come to a fall
(She's) Ready, (I'm) Set, (Let's) Go!

Part One:
It isn't easy to write a poem about anybody
But for you without a doubt to me are somebody.
There are days where I want to miss you
(Again, and Again.)
There are days where I want to kiss you
(Again, and Again.)
I want you in my life for all the right reason,
Hopefully in the future for more than a season,
My mind won't let you go
My heart won't let you go
Like you always say,
You got that effect on people

This is true

When my heart only beats for a few

In this case, it's been for you.

I know that you don't want a man

Or a romantic relationship

But when I see you all I say is damn

I'm willing to be your best companionship

Just someone around as a friend of a guy

No boyfriends? No girlfriends? No titles.

Fine then. I can accept that.

Let me be your main guy

That guy that just holds your shopping bags, buy you drinks, dances with

you and say you want to hang out with me over coffee and chocolate.

Until the time is right

To move up the ladder of your heart

Not ever think of you of only one night

To not lose you and be apart.

Part Two:

Maybe you are right

From our moment last night

One of us might fall for each other.

Guess I must admit it

I like where we are with each other.

Regardless of the Q&A Session to the Thursday Morning Lesson

It may or may not be fate to be together

Even if you are going to make me wait forever

Minus your thought on us going out on one date

Put the petal to the metal

And let me call you special

Just give me a chance

To us maybe crossing the line

With or without the romance

But only if it's the right time.

You say you telling me you innocent

Between us, yeah yeah, I'll go with it.

I see us being Friends with Benefits

But okay, I'll let you think about it

(Pause)

Alright, Alright, Alright, you said no

That doesn't mean I want you to go

I was upset

And you texted don't be sad

And for you, I have too much respect

You didn't leave me and for that part I am glad.

Richmond is only but a short moment of time

And maybe one day over some wine in the light of a city

We can properly hang out and just be friendly.

Part Three:

I give you all of me in pure recognition

Because you've given me pure appreciation

From the playful banter to our witty fights

You're all up in my head

Someone just to talk up all night

Just talking on the bed

Get close and reconnect

Right?

You fear that it might be a bad idea

Since it might lead up to it again

Trust me friend

Though it might make me feel upset,

For you, I honestly agree and respect

Without you in my life, my mind would not be so clear

Or even create a sad tear
As you often tease me
As you often annoy me
Or even question on how to please thee
You really do have that positive effect on people.
I just hope one day you would give me a proper chance.
And before you do the dance to the song Staying Alive,
Don't forget about me after you reach Twenty-Five.

#24 Your Heart for My Soul

The Declaration of Introduction/Chorus:
Sexy lady, you are the Crème de la Crème
When all you do is steal all my gems.
You got me chasing you down like a game of tag
Cause you are as clever as the bear Moneybags.
The Blue Thief that stole my soul,
For now, I'll run and take control
You're the type of woman that likes to throw some shade
I'm the type of man that likes to blow through some babe
If you give me your heart and soul
I'll give you the whole world
Just say that you will be my girl.
(She's) Ready, (I'm) Set, (Let's) Go!

Part One:
Love or lust babe, I cannot decide
You got my heart and mind in a split
Take a hit of your chocolate high
You're the drug that I don't want to quit.
Against the world, you are the perfect distraction
You're a star babe; lights, camera, action
Let me give you the inner passion
You set me free like R&B
You give me life like an angelic harmony
You're the perfect thief.
You stole my heart like a robbery
But against the popular belief
You're the type of woman that likes to throw some shade

I'm the type of man that likes to make a trade.
If you give me your heart and soul
I'll give you the world
Just say that you will be my girl.

Chorus:
Sexy lady, you are the Crème de la Crème
When all you do is steal all my gems.
You got me chasing you down like a game of tag
Cause you are as clever as the bear Moneybags.
You're the Blue Thief that stole my soul,
Without it, I will charge at you and then take control
You're the type of woman that likes to throw some shade
I'm the type of man that likes to make a trade.
If you give me your heart and soul
I'll give you the world
Just say that you will be my girl.

Part Two:
Love has no set age
On when to find it
As we set up the stage
Calling you the (shh)
Spotted you on the side
Come inside my fly ride
As I'm playing some Rick Ross
You know that I'm a Boss
I'm the Master of Romance
When I make that Money Dance
Your heart, sex, and skill I want to go after
Because you get hotter and hotter in each chapter.

You got that L.B.D

That got even got MJ singing P.Y.T

I want you in my life if you stay down for everything

Then call the angels to give you the crown and ring

Chorus:

Sexy lady, you are the Crème de la Crème

When all you do is steal all my gems.

You got me chasing you down like a game of tag

Cause you are as clever as the bear Moneybags.

You're the Blue Thief that stole my soul,

Without it, I will charge at you and then take control

You're the type of woman that likes to throw some shade

I'm the type of man that likes to make a trade.

If you give me your heart and soul

I'll give you the world

Just say that you will be my girl.

Part Three:

As I'm circling around your block

Baby girl, you are the talk of the talk

When I pull up to your spot, you got me in a state of shock

Standing in your physical stance,

Damn girl give me a lyrical chance.

(I'm looking for) someone to ride with

(I'm looking for) someone to fly with

(Even someone) to dive into the sky with

Can you be that one?

Who can get down and have some fun?

I'll take the wheel and you can ride shotgun

As I'm drinking, driving, sipping

My star, you got me tripping

Pardon my wood, he's so far gone.

As the mood changes in the sexy clouds,

Don't you make one sexy sound.

Quiet storm, she's playing the midnight song

Quiet storm, she's wearing her midnight thong

I'll pour us a glass of wine

As we gonna take our time

Take off your clothes and just undress

Cause on your bed we gonna make a hell of a mess.

We toss and turn in the sheets making a swirl

Babe, rock me down into your world

By the end of this song, we won't lose control

Because you already won my heart for my soul.

#25 The Wrong Girl (Unrequited Love)

The (Back) Introduction:

I had no idea this woman would be a game changer for me.

But in a negative way.

But in the end, she made it into the game that put me into bitter shame.

All this time of me chasing her, it would lead me to a dead end.

Worst part? This girl was supposed to be my fri—someone that I cared about.

I wanted her for a relationship as we have been friendly for a bit,

However, the more I gave to her, the less that I got in respect, friendship, and compassion.

So, I asked God what this all meant for someone to put in all the work loving someone when the other is not showing you the same.

This was His answer to me:

Unrequited Love. By definition: 'love that is not openly reciprocated or understood as such by the beloved…"

(She's) a game changer for the worst, (I'm) just a writer for the better, (Let's) Go!

Part One & Two:

All that I ever did for you

All the times that I cared about you

You spat it in my face

All that I ever did for you.

You spat it in my face.

Did you even have some shred of feeling for me?
Did you even have some shred of feelings for me?
Go on, go on and tell the lies about me
When I have the people behind me
But now I will tell the truth about you.
You lead me on with what I did for you and yet you say it wasn't
my intention.
After some time, I finally saw that you were leading me on like a God
Damn fool
That really did get my attention... you simple tool
I started off with the lust, which was a sad motivation for me to do
But then switched it up for your trust because you were much more
than that.
Wanting you and only you back then, but now I'm better off without you.
I wanted to take you out on one date
To see if it was fate,
Sing it JoJo, it was a Little Too Late.
(*It was never in her best interest*)
But nevertheless,
You only saw me as only your mate
Shates!

Part Three & Four:
Maybe it's from your past,
You've been on a man's hiatus,
Maybe you were just moving a bit too fast
Damn you woman, why do you hate us?
Yes, I'm calling you out on the bullshit
I'm just being a realist
As I call you out as a misandrist!

Yes. That line will stir up some controversy
But thank God it's just a testimony!
Honestly, I'm just keeping it real…
I mean seriously,
I'm just expressing out how I feel.
I mean really,
Who are you to judge me?
Who are you to judge me?
Who are you to judge me?

Part Five & Six:
Hold up, hold up, hold up
(Shut the fuck up!)
Hold up, hold up, hold up
(Shut the fuck up!)
How the hell can you be mad at me?
You treated me like a two-faced frenemy
You honestly get off being mean to me
Like some kind of disgusting bliss
But it was only my mind that was taking the piss out of it.
You insulted me in front of my three best friends
(Seriously? Really? Them?)
You've strung me along
For way too long
Like a ninety-minute song.
You tried to run my life and speak for me.
But you have brought me so much misery.
Mistreated me like I was the man that committed the crime
When I was the man who only gave you all my time
Couldn't take it anymore, the verbal pain
So, I wrote it all down to express my pain
So, I wouldn't go insane

But then you ran out into the town and told them my words.

Convincing them of a new side of me that they never heard

But they knew me. The real me. While you created a new side of me

That even you wouldn't believe

Painting me as an enemy

Now I realize that I don't want to take a chance with thee.

Conclusion:

Determination from the goal

That's what you expected from me to you

Appreciation from the soul

That's what I desired from thee.

I'm too far gone from this emotional abuse

Now my heart and mind agree by calling you a simple girl.

I considered you a very close friend,

But now that must come to a bitter end.

After some time has passed,

Just wanting you for you

Man, way to make me feel like who you are. An Ass.

At the end of it all, like poker

I went all in and lost the game.

We failed, we retaliated and proceeds to hurting me in my life.

Thank God Almighty that you are not my wife!

It was all just a big...

(Fuck You!)

It was all just a big...

(Fuck You!)

It was all just a big...

(sigh)

All of this because I went after you...

#26 The Breakup Testimony (Part II): Shattered Memories

Previously on The Breakup Testimony... (Go back to #3)

The (Present) Introduction:

After reading #3, I see that you all got the point
So, let me roll up this... point.
Let me get back to the Breakup Testimony
As this next part of this will be so crazy.

The (Storyline) Declaration of (Introduction):

This is my Reflection Mode:
The love between us has lost its thrill
Shit, that line hurt more than a bullet
The perfect shot to kill
Because she and I no longer will have a moment
Is it wrong to admit that you would miss your S/O?
Let me say this again
Is it wrong to admit that you would miss your S/O?
After the breakup, are you ready to let go?
That one that made you feel that love was possible?
That love was worth fighting for?
Even Love was worth dying for?
Well, I guess from this, not anymore.
I miss the old you
All the times you let me hold you
Touch you, kiss you and even (learned to) love you.
I can only miss you.
But now I have one more thing to say babe and after this,
I will let the story end once and for all
(She's) Gone, (I'm) Accepting, (Let's) Go!

Part One:

Now that time has settled me down

The infatuation for you has finally settled me down

Now tell me what's with the different changes

Because you are looking at me like a stranger girl

Even thinking of me like I'm a danger in this world

And at first, I was all about blaming you

But I've never, ever down to shaming you

(And I'll be damned)

If I didn't say that I had a fault

(And I'll be damned)

When our relationship fell apart

And when I broke your heart

But you still said that you loved me with all your heart

Right from the start.

It's like walking into a house of mirrors

With our romantic things and stuff

Cards, letters, flowers, dolls, and the necklace

Shit, this list is getting harder for this writer

But I have to make one last attempt to make this clearer:

You said that our relationship was not real that way

And I know there were times we both made it feel that way

Even with my words and actions that were sappy

But I know that there were times I made you happy

But now you and I have that vibe that feel so God damn crappy

The bitter tension to the point of awkwardness

Between

us.

Part Two:

As you stand with your new boyfriend,

It's been so long since I said your name

Repeatedly

Because who knew that I would lose my best friend?

And now I'm back to being single again

Now without you in my life

It feels like love has gunned me down

Telling me that I can't turn this shit around

You used to be my four-leaf clover

But now, you just want us to be over.

(Fine)

I can only look back on the Shattered Memories:

The late nights at your place

Playing games like truth or dare

Kissing and the look on your face

That face that said about me, you still care

It was the best time to escape from life

(traveled the bus and rain to see you in the night)

All night into the morning sunrise

Cause of the place that you used to live at

Now you only look at me and say 'so long'

You were once the girl that made me feel glad

But this is more than just a story turned testimony

But now you look at me as an atrocious memory

Now I stand in the Heavenly courts for us to sort it all out

As you once said that if I wanted you back, I would have to fight for

you again

And I would fight anyone, including your feelings to win you back as

my girlfriend.

Part Three:

I can't remember when the skies were so blue

When the love between us was so true

The grass so much greener

But in your mind, I'm getter meaner and meaner

That's far from the truth

I still care about you, you, you.

Since you won't give me your time,

Fuck this shit, I'll accept the crime.

How many times do I have to say sorry?

                                       (I'm sorry)

How many times do I have to say sorry?

                                       (I'm sorry)

I swear to God that this is not becoming an obsession

But I know that in the end that is up to your discretion

I don't want to end things bad between us

I don't want bad blood between us

(I swear, I swear, I swear, I swear)

If you say you forgive me with your voice

(I swear, I swear, I swear, I swear)

I'll give you a better man with a better choice

But if you truly don't want anything to do with me anymore

Then I will accept defeat and will do nothing more

But I wish you everything good in your life

And you will always have a place in my heart.

As promised at the beginning of this story

I will close on the topic of this Testimony

Outro:

And with that, I just have one question while I hold the palm of your hand

Would you ever welcome me if I visit you and only you in _ _ _ _ land?

Bonus round:

Solve this math equation:

$9x-7i > 3(3x-7u)$

#27 Argument (You're Right)

Part One:

All our arguments
As we go at it all day and all night
All our resentments
Do you want me gone and take flight?
What is the point of us here?
When all we do is shout and give roundabouts...
Where do you and I stand dear?
Let me make myself clear
I believe that these are fair questions
Before one of us drops the execution
Let me beat you to the punch...
I drop my ring in front of you
Grabbed my keys, speeding out of the driveway
Yes, I don't want to front, but I was playing Trey
Sick of Playing Hard, fighting really to even stay
Windows down, music blaring
Drowning out the thought of you
But to no avail; heart plus mind equals you
Five times you're blowing up my phone
Calling me up asking me to come home
This is not a moment of defeat; but I decide to retreat
Put the ring back on my finger, but no one is a winner
Back in the bed and neither of us can stand as just
Should we just stop and just bite the dust?
You know that I don't want you to leave
So, can we try and stay right here please?

Chorus:

Babe, I'll just agree, you can have it

Yeah, you're right, (all day) you're right (let's play)

Babe, I'll just agree, you can have it

Yeah, you're right (all night), you're right (just stay)

(Alright?)

Part Two:

Oh great, here we go again

Seeing you less as a friend

As we still go at it from night to day

I'm in your face to feel superior

What more do you and I have to say?

You're in my face to be inferior

Holy shit woman, just go away

All I hear is accusation turn into bullets

The neighbors, yeah, they heard it

Police raided my house and had me arrested

72 hours later, they let me go…

Best friend waiting for me with a salutation

Like Charlie did for Hank on Califoniation

Driving home to a girl who has one concern

Will we last enough to even stay and learn?

Or should we simply let our bridges burn?

Chorus:

Babe, I'll just agree, you can have it

Yeah, you're right, (all day) you're right (let's play)

Babe, I'll just agree, you can have it

Yeah, you're right (all night), you're right (just stay)

(Alright?)

Part Three:
I know that I haven't done you right
(I'm a jerk, but you are also a jerk)
Give me one more chance for the night
(I know that we can make it work)
Do you remember when we acted like kids?
Laughed hard and stayed up all night long
I don't ever want to see you gone
I know that you want love and respect
I'll give you a new man with no regrets
All I want from you is trust and appreciation
So, I can say that you are my destination

Chorus:
Babe, I'll just agree, you can have it
Yeah, you're right, (all day) you're right (let's play)
Babe, I'll just agree, you can have it
Yeah, you're right (all night), you're right (just stay)
(Alright?)

#28 Split/Second

The Declaration of Introduction:

Dear readers,

Have you seen her?

Have you seen this girl?

This girl is truly the talk of this metropolis world.

She's deception's best cousin, but on the good side of the family.

Convincing and temptation is one of her finest arts. As well
as Conviction.

The appearance of an angel, the intellection of a genius and the voice of
a goddess.

She has the heart of gold and her mind sharper than a razor blade.

Other guys try to take her down, slander her down.

However, before she turns anonymous, she was so well known, the people
behind her would shut them down in a heartbeat. Calling them liars
and haters.

Now she reappears in the spotlight. For just one night.

Like a mirror, I met her and her sexy side and like my heart, I'm split.

(She's) Ready, (I'm) Set, (Let's) Go.

Part One:

In the heart of the bright metropolis,

She's the only one who people call anonymous.

People try so hard to Miranda her,

People try so hard to slander her,

But she's as good as the Flanders.

First encounter and it felt like a twister,

Tonight, in the club, I don't want to miss her
She's got me shaken and stirred
Call it Mixology.
Stirring my feeling and thoughts
Call it Psychology
10 out of 10, you are top quality
Tonight, I want you to have all of me.
Against your friends, I'm sensing some jealousy
Even though you act like a mystery.
That's why you are written in this Testimony.

Part Two:
As she stays mysterious
How can she stay so mysterious?
Sweats of pool of being delirious
She keeps me all night
As she swims in my mind frame
She's so divine in this ocean game
I've lost track of time,
So, she said to drink and unwind
I've lost track of time.
So, she said smoke on this blunt
Damn girl, I don't want to front
She's the perfect remedy
Like this perfect melody.
As love and lust leave me in a havoc
Common (Man), I've seen the Light
She leaves me in wonder like magic
She's not the type to do just for the night
Bitten from this love bug
Smitten from this love drug

I'm chasing you in a heart's rush
Because you are my heart's crush.
No strings attached.

(Wait. No. Screw That.)

I just met your second side tonight
Don't cuff her as your wife
She said to give her the time of her life
Can't waste no time
I'm kissing her waistline.
Sweet Valentine.
It's you, me, and her
As the night truly unfurl
Say yes to be with me
As we move on to Part Three.

Part Three:
The Smooth

Bandit Angelic Vibes

We're swimming in our bed of lies
Strumming

down

our

double

alibi

This drug is fleeting
Kissing her and you
Yes, yes, yes… I'm cheating.
Damn you lust, I'm just a human being.
As she dances on me in this chair
You both look good in your underwear
How can I even compare?

Looked into her eyes, can't give her no less of me
Robbed me for the night, she got the best of me
At the end of the night, kept her and my love affair
At the end of the night, who's to say life isn't fair?
At the end of the night, it was only a game world
Cause in the very end, they were the same girl.

#29 Beyond the Night (Part One)

Part One:
Girl, the way you look tonight
On a clear blue night with the silver moon
This night is feeling so right
We stand together in the room
All glowed up by the open windows,
As we are blended into the night like shadows
Your eyes glow like green emeralds
Your dress shines like a ruby
Great Gatsby vibes like Fitzgerald
Looking at you like you are the one for me
The room was so cold that I had to shiver
I said I just want to kiss her
She said come closer
She took me into a new world of pleasure and pain
(Let me further explain…)
First, it was full of the pleasure; us simply chilling and kissing
Then it was to the point of pain of us missing and killing
Man, this scene is starting to get boring
(Damn, what are we even doing?)
She said let's go beyond the night
Take one with me and we can go beyond the flight
We took one pill, one sip, up the thrill, start the trip
Feeling so sedated, yet so elevated

Bridge:

Then when we got into the bed and took a detour

Into doing something we have never done before

As we now are about to enter the darkness

Chorus:

She said

Let's go beyond the night

She said

Let's glow as the sparks ignite

She said

Open your eyes and look at me

Tell me that you want me

Don't get lost in the sight

Take my hand and it will be alright

Let's go beyond the night

Part Two:

First round was tough on the head

But to her, it wasn't enough… so instead

She said let's go beyond the night again

Take one with me and we can go beyond the flight again

Another pill and another sip

That's our New Addiction

Before we got into the next trip

That's our New Edition

Can you Stand the Rain?

Will you take all my pain?

(You'll take mine and I'll take yours)

While we are on this floor

Fighting with our demons of our inner darkness

As we're surfing on the sea of calmness

Contemplating on a high mind
This is our moment to shine
Stroke back your hair while you lay down so bare
As both of you looked so good in your underwear
But for a Split/Second, I knew that it was you
As we kept going around and around like a typhoon
She fucks like a devil in this bed
Making me feel lighter and lighter like a balloon
But she came like an angel in this bed

Bridge:
Then when we got into the bed and took a detour
Into doing something we have never done before
As we now are about to enter the darkness

Chorus:
She said
Let's go beyond the night
She said
Let's glow as the sparks ignite
She said
Open your eyes and look at me
Tell me that you want me
Don't get lost in the sight
Take my hand and it will be alright
Let's go beyond the night

Part Three:
You are all in my veins
(And I kinda like it)
And you got me feeling insane
(And I kinda like it)

With you, I just want to smoke the light away
With you, I just want to joke the night away
She said go one last round with me
(Beyond the night)
She said go one last round with me
(Beyond the flight)
This last round you will feel it. Guarantee.
So, she went into her drawer and doubled our prescription
Damn, that was my worst decision
I don't want to lose her in this hallucination
As she hit me with the double interrogation
Will you fight with me out of the darkness?
Will you be light in my sea of calmness?

(Hold up. Hold up. Do you hear that?)

Part Four:
My Heart is slowing down
(And I'm trying, I'm trying)
To get up
My Heart is going down
(And I'm dying, I'm dying)
That's fucked up
One flash and then I heard a crash
Like a flat line on ice
But God thought twice
For me to be in paradise
He simply said: No. Not yet.
It's probably for the best
My body was so cold that I had a shiver
She said come closer and kiss her
But from her kiss, we were beyond alright
Because she brought me back to life
All that from us going Beyond the Night.

#30 The Guilty Man's Confession

The Guilty Man's Sinful (Introduction) Prayer:

Father, Father, Father God

Please forgive me for I have committed this sin

Father, Father, Father God

I'm just feeling so odd, both outside and in

I say that women are always mean

Women are always mad.

Never making any man glad

You ever wonder why?

Well men, there are things that are to us unseen

Girls can be sad.

(I know. They have feelings too. How do we forget that as men?)

From the action and words of those men,

That's all they ever heard from them.

I'm a filthy man outside and in

That's why I'm writing this true story.

To confess my deepest sin

The Guilty Man's Sinful Testimony.

(She's) Praying, (I'm) Repenting, (Let's) Go!

The (Guilty Man's Sinful) Past:

I used to be that guy

Who acted so coy

When actually was as organic as soy.

Pure man.

Thinking like a man, but acting like a boy

Flirting with women

Didn't care if it messed up their world

Some said yes to this

Most women said no to this.

One and done

Just having fun.

Fast words and quick lines,

Her heart's in a compromise

She said he's such a nice guy

When I knew those words were just a lie

Fast words and quick lines,

Her heart's in a compromise

Until one false line and I made her cry.

Damn. Why did I commit that crime?

Not my best

Just have me under arrest.

Inside my heart,

Right from the start

It wasn't right.

This isn't what a relationship is supposed to be

This isn't what a relationship is supposed to be

Loving and caring for women who make men better

A good man is my true character

No lie or lay

I swear to God

But you only laugh and say...How odd!

For Fuck Sake!

I made a mistake!

For Fuck Sake!

I made a mistake!

Feeling so strange,

This man wants to make a change

For you and not be like those other guys

Again, no lie.

Please believe me

The (Guilty Man's Sinful) Present:

I caused more damage than a hurricane,

Worse than that, I caused her so much pain

Making her feel so worthless.

How can I be so heartless?

I wasn't the main guy to cause her pain

Just the final man who has made that claim

What I see now is revealing

It's such a bitter feeling

This girl had feelings.

Shit line.

That's why I'm trying to fix my crime.

So, call me names, sure even an asshole

I'm not the bitter man that you met in the past (so)

Please don't cut me off this fast

I admit to my mistaken remark as a man

As we all make it as only being humans.

For that, God… damn… this man.

I just want to be in your friend plans.

Show you that I am not those others who made you sad

But still be that friend who made you laugh, smile, and feel glad.

My character you can honestly destroy if you feel like this

No telling after this if you call me or this apology shit

I truly don't even deserve to write about you

But I'm not trying to give the round about you.

Then I cried,

Without you in my life, it's worthless.

All I'm asking is for your forgiveness.

Then she said,

Practice all that of what you preach

No more words or any of this speech

The (Guilty Man's) Future (Lesson):

Attention all men,

Take the life lesson from a friend.

Watch what you say to a lady

Because they could give you the time of the day

Again, if you say what you say.

Given from a filthy man,

It's so strange man

I'm a changed man!

I'm a changed man!

A man who wants to take a woman by the hand

And take the stand

We ALL make mistakes…

But it shows admirations to make the change

And do what it takes…

For forgiving my past

For understanding my present

For trusting me in the future

From my past of being such a filthy man

To God pardoning my sins as a Guilty man

**(#31 & #32 are intentionally missing.
Just turn to the next page).**

#33 Love Well Spent

The Declaration of Introduction:
Material things
Or
Physical things
It does not matter to me when it comes to you.
As we go through the stages of the friendship
You deserve the best in between this life
To us maturing into a romantic relationship
Even before I considered you as my wife.
I'll give you my all to the very last cent
Because for you, it would be Love Well Spent.
(She's) Priceless, (I'm) Timeless, (Let's) Go

Part One: My Best (Girl) Friend:
First things First,
Girl, you're the realist
You're my Day One to the end
Girl, you're the realist
I don't want our relationship to end.
Spending time and money on you.
Spending wine and energy on you.
First guy on your list to run for fun
All day and all night, I'm number one
Never a dull moment in your or my life.
I never had to buy your friendship
Or use this poem as a token to a relationship
You're worth more than anything money can buy
And I'm that best friend that will never lie

You're a true celebrity that represents
Anything you want, I'll spend it to the last cent
Anything for you will be Love Well Spent.

Part Two: My Girlfriend

For so long babe,
I want you like a rare R&B song babe.
It was hard for me to believe
That someone like you would like someone like me.
I want to shower you with some poems.
I want to shower you with some flowers.
I want to shower you with some gifts.
Took you out on a couple of dates
Since now I can now you my best mate
Not because of what you did for me
Because you said that you like me like me.
You call me a perfect gentle(boy)friend
Like a jacket over a puddle,
I want to lay down with you.
To us in bed and I get to cuddle with you
You love my humor and call it funny
Spending overtime with you like money
You're a true celebrity that represents
Anything you want, I'll spend it to the last cent
Anything for you will be Love Well Spent.

Part Three: My Fiancée

You make my heart boiling for you.
Babe, I want to start spoiling you
Lace you up with the best kind of fashion
Taste you up with the best kind of passion
Love, sex, whatever

You can have my endeavor.

I have you all to myself

Yes. I'm selfish.

Like Michael Jackson, I Can't Help It.

We can go around town

I want you to shine with me like a crystal

Like an artist to a singer

I think it's time for us to be official

Like in the Wedding Ringer.

I will get down on one knee

Like Jay-Z did to Beyoncé

To ask you to be my fiancée

You kiss me and say yes with your heart and mentally,

Possibly revealing you as my Heaven and Reality?

Part Four: My (Future) Wife

As we stand between God and our friends

This love between us will never ever end.

God, I'm about to marry my best (girl) friend.

Fresh cut fade with a black suit and tie

White dress with sparkles around you with an angelic glow

Girl, the way you look so fly

You are the true Miss London Star of this wedding show!

Before I seal our final payment of this relationship

Let me make myself clear

From our first kiss to the friendship

That turned into a romantic relationship

You're a true celebrity that represents

Anything you want, I'll spend it to the last cent

Anything for you will be Love Well Spent.

#34 Our Moment in Time

Part One:
It's a bore without her during the weekday
Monday through Thursday
But on Friday
When we link up,
We can party and we can drink from our cup
Rocking with her like we share the same birthday
On Friday,
It's a calm day
Partying all night like it's payday
Never want our moment together to end
Let's move it to the weekend

Part Two:
Buying and eating Krispy Kremes
Watching movies or making funny Memes
To Saturday night, we hit the club
Acting and dancing like little kids
To all my boys, I called (on you) dibs,
You giggled and said shut up
Acting all grown up
In this big world
You're like no other girl.
Superwoman you play the role
I'm the beat to her R&B Soul.
Our friendship is so prime
This is our moment in time.

#35 Stay or Go?

The Declaration of Introduction:
Should I Stay or should I Go?
On the definition of Love, no one really knows
Should I stay or should I go?
This is the first side of this flow.
(She's) Ready, (I'm) Set, (Let's) Go

Part One:
On our good days,
She makes me feel so well
When we do the talking and kissing
And simply reminiscing.
On our bad days
I'm taking so many L's
From us barking and hissing
I rather stay in Hell.
Some days she gets me on the steady thinking
On the days where we both lied
Other days she gets me on the heavy drinking
On the days where we both cried
Feeling like our relationship just died
To the point where we both run and hide
Why do we treat each other like foes?
I just want to love you from your head to your toes.
And I know that you want to do the same
For both of us to not treat love like a game

You only said hold me
Cause without me, you would feel so lonely
I don't want to stray from you
I have to make a move and choose
To either stay or go from you.

Part Two:
That old line that everybody knows:
The heart knows what it wants
But not this time.
Because my mind is in denial
(So, go ahead and tell her)
So instead, it puts you on trial
(So here comes the defender)
The Angel on my shoulder
Telling me to kiss and hold her
But the Devil can be loud as Hell
Telling me that we will not prevail
Dragging me into a place of tears
(The woman that I fell for)
Showing me how to face all my fears
(The woman that I would leave Hell for)
Making everything seem so clear
Such a hard decision now
Until she read the inscription of our sacred vows
"To forgive the past and live in the now"
But now we are standing here in the clouds
Where yelling at each other is the only sound
What the hell are we going to do now?

Part Three:

Given our love is in so many directions
Please let me ask you this question
Should we even stay down and be together?
(Yes)
Do you see us saying I Do and being forever?
(Yes)
Cause at the end of the day, sometimes I don't even have a clue
But I know that I want to be with you and stay true
Cause we both started off as best friends
Even though we fight every now and again
We said that we would love each other until the end
And we know that life can get messy
But you stayed with me
Through Heaven and Reality
I want to love you eternally
There will be days
That I will want you to say leave me
Cause of the way that we fight
But in reality
I rather be talking and kissing late into the night
Until everything between us is alright.

#36 Time's Running Out...

The (Backstory) Declaration of Introduction:

No matter what time does to us
Good, bad, or indifferent
For better or worse
Against Time's Cures
I will always love you until we run out of time

The Declaration of Introduction:

You and I have so much time together
(So, let's marinate in this moment)
You and I have so much time together
(So, let's celebrate in this moment)
Against all these girls, you're the rarest find
That's why I'm so glad to say that you are mine.
Through all my infidelities
You still love me through our memories
Through all my bullshit
Mentally, sexually, physically
You still love me good, bad, and indifferently.
From being my best friend to my girlfriend,
I don't want this moment between us to end
(So, she said) stop the clock
(So, she said) let's go back to when we met on the block
(She's) Ready, (I'm) Set, (Let's) Go!

Part One:
Without a wake-up call,
The Sands of Time
Won't let me even unwind,
God, the fear of it all.
(Let it all fall)
(Let it all fall)
From the girl who played me like a song,
To the memories of everyone I knew is now long gone.
Too tired to mentally move on.
Until you walked into my life
And made it alright.
You got me thinking
The sweetest feeling
Like a breeze on the ocean horizon before the storm.
She made a better me
Ne-Yo, I found my Integrity.
She got me falling in love for the first time
Damn. Is this all real?
The way that you make me feel?
You got my face grinning when we are kissing
Hurry up babe. The clock is still ticking.

Chorus:
Tick Tock, Tick Tock
Time is running me down
Tick Tock, Tick Tock
Time is gunning me down
Oh babe, I can't believe that you are next to me
As we're kissing under these docks
You got my heart under key and lock
Go on babe girl and start the clock
Let's love it out like Time's Running Out.

Part Two:

Like Big Ben striking chimes in the Tower

I'm ringing you every minute every second every hour.

This is every man's decision, hoping and wishing for you to stay.

I've only got eight minutes left to change the pace

I've only got eight minutes left to change the race

Against time.

From Monday to Friday,

Seeing you almost every day

Loving you from your screaming and moaning

In this bedroom that is filled with wonder and space

You've got my heart in a pure chase and into outer space

Your kisses, your hugs, your intimate sex, and your affection

Has gotten my full attention.

All I want to do is love you and please you

Like a goddess

She said in this bed, you don't have to be so modest.

Just love me down and give me some time.

And I will have you screaming mine.

Damn. Is this all real?

The way that you make me feel?

You got my face grinning when we are kissing

Hurry up babe. The clock is still ticking.

Chorus:

Tick Tock, Tick Tock

Time is running me down

Tick Tock, Tick Tock

Time is gunning me down

Oh babe, I can't believe that you are next to me

As we're kissing under these docks

You got my heart under key and lock

Go on babe girl and start the clock
Let's love it out like Time's Running Out.

Part Three:
Babe, I think it's time we run down the clock
(Tick Tock)
(Tick Tock)
How we first met from the block. (Yeah Jenny)
It's never too late
To escape from Time's fate
Never on that nine to five clocks
Dealing pounds for pounds on the block
I'm such a hustle man like Ghost on Power
Shine babe girl like you the host of the hour
With you on my side
Through life, you're my only ride or die
The world can be ours
As long as we are together
Promise we will live forever

Chorus:
Tick Tock, Tick Tock
Time is running me down
Tick Tock, Tick Tock
Time is gunning me down
Oh babe, I can't believe that you are next to me
As we're kissing under these docks
You got my heart under key and lock
Go on babe girl and start the clock
Let's love it out like Time's Running Out.

#37 Sex Attack (Prelude)

The (Sexy) Declaration of Introduction:
I hope you are ready tonight
(So, take it off slowly)
I hope you are ready tonight
(So, take it off slowly)
From the way you look like that
From the front to the back
I'm about to have a Sex attack.
But before we get to that,
Let me take it all in with a drink in my hand
I hope that tonight that you will understand.
When you walk in like an authority,
She croons to Start this testimony
(She's) Ready, (I'm) Set, (Let's) Go!

Part One:
From your L.B.D,
Why are you teasing me tonight?
Babe,
Do you think that this is pleasing me right?
Actions speaks louder than words.
A couple of drinks, a couple of disses.
A couple of winks, a couple of kisses.
You got my mind wondering what's under there
You walk into my room
As you're stripping down to your sexy underwear
Just to spend the night
The Swirling Scent of Alcohol and Perfume all over your body

Sit on my lap and let me kiss down

I still want you, you, you

You do a dance for me

To tease me when I want to please you

Tie my hands behind my back

Let me see you again from the front to the back

As my body wants your body for this Sex Attack.

Chorus:
I hope you are ready tonight

(So, take it off slowly)

I hope you ready tonight

(So, take it off slowly)

From the way you look like that

From the front to the back

All dressed in black

I'm about to have a Sex Attack.

Part Two:
You gave me the old saying

Before we began the role playing

Wear the glove or no love tonight

Alright babe.

Let me wrap him up

Before I lift you up

So, I can take you down

Go round, after round, after round on her and taste the sound

Of your body calling me out

On your pleasure that's greater than any treasure

Let me lick you up again and again

Let me pick you up again and again

Against these walls while I'm kissing your neck and giving you my all

As I look at your sex face
You're telling me don't change the pace
Grind me down to my favorite song
101 on the 101… making this so easy
Blow me down until my mind is gone
I'll make your body say that you want me like I want you.
Let me see you again from the front to the back
As my body wants your body for this Sex Attack.

Chorus:
I hope you are ready tonight
(So, take it off slowly)
I hope you ready tonight
(So, take it off slowly)
From the way you look like that
From the front to the back
All dressed in black
I'm about to have a Sex attack.

Part Three:
You've really taken me by surprise
You're the truth and the whole truth
No lies.
Got you screaming, moaning, and groaning
Until the next morning.
Give me your trust
(If only for one night)
Give me your lust
(If only for one night)
It's alright.
Now stare back at the mirror
Let my body feel your body

Let this moment be even clearer.

Be my sex memory (wait a minute…) Be my best fantasy

Love me down and lift me up

From the way you look like that

Let me see you again from the front to the back

As my body wants your body for this Sex Attack.

Sexy Outro:

What more can I say?

With or without the lingerie

Your body is your best attack

The best Sex Attack.

#38 Don't Play Fair (Bonus)

The Declaration of Introduction:

The record is playing in the background. Two friends laughing over drinks. The girl looks at the clock and slowly gets up. The guy bewildered clears his throat. This is their conversation.

Mr. Amatory: Hey. Hey. Where are you going?

Sara: I should be getting home tonight. I've been with you all day.

Mr. Amatory: Babe, like this record song playing, *Don't Stray Away…*

Sara: Quoting the Jazz Artist Marcus Anderson?

Mr. Amatory: You got that one right tonight. Come one babe. I don't want to drink alone tonight. I want you to stay…

Sara: Really Mr. Amatory. I should be going home…

Mr. Amatory: Where's the fire dear? Just have one more drink with me. I'll make your favorite…

Sara: The Bentley?

Mr. Amatory: You must really know me.

Mr. Amatory goes back into the kitchen to make the drink.
A few minutes later, he returns and hands Sara the glass drink.

Mr. Amatory: What do you think?

Sara: Better than your last batch. Thank you.

Mr. Amatory smiles and goes over and switches the song.
He goes over to Sara and extend his hands.

Mr. Amatory: Come on. Dance with me.

Sara laughs and takes Mr. Amatory's hand.

Sara: You are so buzzed. Come sit down with me. It's getting cold right now.

Mr. Amatory: You sure?

Sara: Yes. You are in no dancer mode right now. I'll stay one more hour and I'll leave.

Mr. Amatory: Alright. (Mr. Amatory sits down and gets close to Sara). Guess we shall get close.

Sara: And before we get there, I'll take out my phone and we shall take our pose.

Mr. Amatory: (She's) Ready, (I'm) Set, (Let's) Go!

Part One:
It's getting late
(The record's still spinning)
It's getting late
We still be talking, laughing, drinking, and thinking
On the memories of our past
Babe, don't want to move to fast
But the Brandy is still making me buzzed.
Oh wait, that's just my phone.

Let me shut it off

Let's just be alone.

She's got me thinking of us being more than being friendly

The way she's looking at me, she looks like she's ready.

She whispers into my ear

Babe, don't leave me alone

I want you to stay here

All in my home

She's got me Swimming in My Conscience

My feelings for her

(From our past conversation)

My feelings for her

(Filled with fast temptation)

She said let's have some fun

Baby…

Maybe, we should take it slow

But she said she was ready to glow

Giving me the green light

But does this feel right?

(As she's coming closer and closer)

She's got my heart beating like a drummer

(As she's coming closer and closer)

She's got me feeling hotter than Summer

She kissed me once and said I don't usually play this way

And tonight, I want you to want me to stay

You're not those guys who says 'I just want to fuck you'

But to you, but to you… I just want to trust you.

But given how we are, buzzed and all

You might have me for more than one night.

I'm gonna give you the ball

If you can do this right

Chorus:

You Don't Play Fair

(You don't, you don't, you don't)

You Don't Play Fair

(You don't, you don't, You Don't)

When you wear that dress

It makes me say that I'm impressed

When you wear that lingerie

You know that I really want you to stay

When you get naked

You know that I can't take it

Your body's so sophisticated

You know that I can't take it

I put my hand up in surrender

You Don't Play Fair

Part Two:

Babe, you are such a tease and a part of me likes it

You don't play fair

When you wear that type of bra and underwear (set)

I want to be like Musiq and Takeyouthere (bet)

Babe, don't feel so anxious

I know that you been so patient

We can go all the way

From night to day

If you want me to stay

Baby, Baby, Baby.

Your body is driving me crazy, crazy, crazy

So many things I want to do to you

Cause I'm buzzing on some Queen B

Feeling so Crazy in Love that I want to Cater 2 U

Let me Dance 4 U

Lay you down on the bed like Operation

Where you wait here in anticipation

I want to play with your body

Live out all your fantasies

While you want some privacy

Where I kiss your body from head to toe

Place my hand behind your back and hold you down

Make your body go around, around, and around

Until I go downtown and moan out the perfect sound

Chorus:

You Don't Play Fair

(You don't, you don't, you don't)

You Don't Play Fair

(You don't, you don't, You Don't)

When you wear that dress

It makes me say that I'm impressed

When you wear that lingerie

You know that I really want you to stay

When you get naked

You know that I can't take it

Your body's so sophisticated

You know that I can't take it

I put my hand up in surrender

You Don't Play Fair

Part Three:

She said I won't let this fire burn down

As she gets up and said her turn to get down

Like a storm with the rain and thunder

She said let me take you over till we both slumber

We gonna get it all over my bed

Climb on top and don't stop
Switch it up and lay you down
Babe, scratch my back
Like I'm under a Sex Attack
I'll scream your name like I forgot it
Let's push it to the limit and go Super Sonic
You'll have us coming…right back for each other
Best lover when we can do this under the covers
Don't see why we have to quit this
You know that we can't resist this
Let's give into it

Chorus:
You Don't Play Fair
(You don't, you don't, you don't)
You Don't Play Fair
(You don't, you don't, You Don't)
When you wear that dress
It makes me say that I'm impressed
When you wear that lingerie
You know that I really want you to stay
When you get naked
You know that I can't take it
Your body's so sophisticated
You know that I can't take it
I put my hand up in surrender
You Don't Play Fair

Part Four:
Truthfully, I know you Don't Play Fair
Playfully, I know that you don't even care
All these girls were so hard to please

So, in my life, they had to take their leave

Then you came into my life and made it more interesting

Between you and me, we have a good thing

And we can do it whenever

That's what makes our thing so much better

So, let's get acquainted

(Before we get too faded)

So, let's get acquainted

(Before we get too faded)

Take me up to your room

Rev me up like Vroom-Vroom

While you do my favorite move

Rocket 2 the Moon

I'll be on my best while we play in these sheets

And in return

You can have my heart and these Pink Rose Beats.

Chorus:

You Don't Play Fair

(You don't, you don't, you don't)

You Don't Play Fair

(You don't, you don't, You Don't)

When you wear that dress

It makes me say that I'm impressed

When you wear that lingerie

You know that I really want you to stay

When you get naked

You know that I can't take it

Your body's so sophisticated

You know that I can't take it

I put my hand up in surrender

You Don't Play Fair

#39 (Like A) Virgin (True Testimony)

Part One:
Such anticipation
So much expectation
Pure temptation
As we lay down on your bed
We can just lay down and cuddle down
I promise that we won't get into any trouble now
But a man has needs and a woman has needs
So, who are we as humans to ignore our needs?
I know that you gonna lose your man now
(So, I might be out of line)
Cause he doesn't put it down
(Like every (other) single time)
So, tell me why keep him around?
Take him out and slide me in now
I'll kiss you on your neck as a starter
Then make you wish that I would hit it harder
Five hours before the midnight train
But I have to stay in my lane
So tonight, I'll make you feel like a virgin again

Part Two:
I know that this is not your first time
That you came
But I'mma make it feel like the first time
That's my promise to our game
Cup my hands in your breast and kiss them
Make my lips say that I will miss them

Make your body feel so much better and better

Get you wetter and wetter

When I'm licking your fines pallet

That's the taste of sex

Whenever you want it, you can have it

Nothing but the best!

Let's go by your mirror

I want to see your body clearer

Feel your curves of your body while you back that up and drop it down

You don't want me to take it there

I guess that's fair

Then you said fuck it, I don't care

Strip down to your underwear

Let me see your bum

Because you are so worth the time

Just say for tonight that your body is mine

Give me that feeling, and I'll give you one more line

Part Three:

Is me asking you for another round a little insane?

But I have to catch the midnight train

I don't want to leave and make this a one and done

One for the money, two for the show

Let me finger you real slow before I have to go

Just to give you a quick smile

Feeling inside you to get to the limit

No rest as you said to taste your breast

Long sighs for about ten minutes

Unleash your waterfall

I'll kiss you against the wall

Turn you around against the wall

Drop it low and grind on it one more time

You got your body on my mind
All I want to do is press rewind
And do that one more time
I wish I could fuck you off
But my watch goes off
I gotta catch that midnight train
I don't want to bounce,
(but I have to go)
I don't want to bounce,
(but I have to go)
Cause he's about to overflow
Don't say it's the last time we will have sex
But in case it is, read this outro of our text

Outro Text Message:
23:59
Mr. Amatory: Hey… did I leave my wallet in your place. JK. Founds
it anyway
Girl: I was gonna look for it
Mr. Amatory: Lol. Thanks though Love. For a good night
Girl: No, thank you.

#40 Venus Girl (Part One)

The Declaration of Introduction:
The nights grew so cold and I couldn't stand it
Living in this old world of this planet
Now…Granted
The earth girls who came to Mars did everything for the men
Both parties felt no shame
When they came to me
They were the same
The love that they shared wasn't their first
And that just made the shit even worse
When they left, it didn't feel right
Even though they only came every other night.
I had to stay tough through it
But my heart had enough of this shit
I fell on my knees and began to pray, pray, pray
(For a Woman of Worth)
To find someone that would take me away, away, away
(From these Women of Earth)
And lo and behold
She came down from Heaven
And all I can say is Good Lord!
Rolling the dice to get a seven
I wrote this story for you like a genius girl
This one is called Venus girl
(She's) Out of this world, (I'm) a Writer, (Let's) Go!

Part One:

She was everything I prayed her up to be
To be that girl that can make me feel so happy
She saw no man before her worthy
But I needed to be like Faith and make her my Legacy
Like the definition of Venus
You stand with class and beauty
Like the perfection of a genius
Your intellectual words move me
You have all the best features
Even if we are two different creatures
When I am with you
It feels like I'm on a whole new planet
The brains, the heart, and the beauty
For the life of thee
My heart can't stand it
The way you took over my world
In that one moment of time and space
I want you to be my number one girl
To love and kiss you all over the place
Coming from the planet so far
You make me feel like a star
And I'm just a simple man from Mars.

Part Two:

Every day and every night
You only come and see me and only me
Every day and every night
You are the reason I'm no longer lonely
The rest of the world we can ignore it
As we lay in this bed and just fade into orbit
Like the sun and the moon
Rotate around me until high noon
From the sex to the guitar
I want you to take it far
'Till we see the stars
And we go again and again
Breathe for the both of us
Like oxygen
Let's speed down this lane
Like nitrogen
Again, and again and again
Let me take you all in
You can rock that old beat
A lady in the street and a freak in the sheet
You can still rock my beat
Come over in your Trench Coat
Wake up in the morning
I'll treat you to some French Toast

Part Three:

When it comes to these Earth girls

They don't even have that worth girl

As you hold me down like 702

No Doubt

Crowing you like Miss Universe

I need you like I need this verse

You came and took away the loveless curse

All those other girls were so strange to me

But you made me want to change for thee

You are the woman in my whole galaxy

And when push came to shove

You went above and beyond to make me so happy

(You are such a genius girl)

And that is why you will be the woman that I will love

(Venus girl)

#41 True Luxury

Part One:
Let's start with the basic call
The Women, The Whiskey, The Music
My goal to taste them all
Right hand to God, that's therapeutic
Never letting my palate fail
Got to move faster than a snail
Let's see where this story will entail
She got me frozen up like ice on the wrist
She rewrote my life like twice on this twist
Cause of the way she does that stance
I have to make my move in one chance
So, I took her out on a date
To see if she was to be my fate
Looking in her eyes, I only saw hope
Rather, I saw only glee
Racing down this moment like a slope
She said I was only meant for thee

Chorus:
They say the best things in life are free
So loving you must be a true luxury
You put your whole trust in me
Even when I only had lust for me
You made life so much more to see
Making my like so balanced
Like harmony
Matter of fact, turning it into a reality

This must be true serendipity
True Luxury

Part Two:
For Goodness Sake,
I could be roaming with honeys like I'm in the famous colosseum
From Time, I'm singing like Drake
But I don't need to do those things
When you are the woman that can give me everything
From you knowing how to cut a rug
To your touch, your kiss, and your hugs
I don't need a woman to act sassy
I need a woman that act classy
At any time and in any style
It's my pleasure to make you smile
In public, you work at a level so effectively
In private, you work at a level so heavenly
The way you make those moves towards your destiny
You are a woman of value
And to God, I say thank you
I want to spend all my time with you
No matter the cost because you are a dream come true!

Chorus:
They say the best things in life are free
So, loving you must be a true luxury
You put your whole trust in me
Even when I only had lust for me
You made life so much more to see
Making my like so balanced
Like harmony
Matter of fact, turning it into a reality

This must be true serendipity
True Luxury

Part Three:
Though life may become expensive
Let's live it up because we only have one life to give
"Take what you can, give nothing back"
Yeah. Great quote Jack.
(So, forget the cost)
We're not taking any loss
(So, forget the cost)
Because I want to see you floss
Because you my lady… is a boss
So, let's toast it up to your success
To you, to you, a woman of finesses
A woman of value
And to God, I say Thank you
Thank you
For bringing this girl in my life to give me harmony
While she gets from me the definition of true luxury.

Chorus:
They say the best things in life are free
So, loving you must be a true luxury
You put your whole trust in me
Even when I only had lust in me
You made life so much more to see
Making my life so balanced
Like harmony
Matter of fact, turning it into a reality
This must be true serendipity
True Luxury

#42 Half a Heart

Part One:

God, since when did Love become a tournament?
None of these girls want something permanent
Most of the guys just made them experiment
Now I look for something that people call an illusion
Something that's real, something to feel, no confusion
Shaping you as that girl that I will always be musing
Sexing strong until we both feel like cruising
(Preach)
But the last one got me on a team that's losing
All her feelings went up and left that night
She did all the talking with no time for a turn
She took her keys and made the front tires burn
The radio just had to play that song by Blackstreet
As I screamed Don't Leave Me on that street.

Part Two:

Way to go London Star,
Time to buy a brand-new car
And go to a someplace very far
Pulled up to H-Town and became a Part Time lover
Against my feelings, it's time to go undercover
Went inside the strip club where women were the distraction
Met this beautiful dancer that just wanted some interaction
I comply and let her start her dance.

Her body smoother than a Bentley
Her Hips swayed like palm trees,
Skin darker than some whisky
Her wild ambitions like safaris
She said that all these guys are irreverent
I said I just want to be insignificant (Yeah, that's a lie)
She said that I was different (from the other guys)
Her words were Magnificent
I said to her to stop the dance
She said just to give her a chance
I said that I don't want to give my whole heart to be broken
She said just trust me with half of my heart as a token
I guess it's a half of a start

Part Three:
I'm such of a bitch turned in a cur
I couldn't really be with her
She is everything that every man would pray for
But I could never honestly level up to stay so
I had to play ghost and disappear from her
Instead of giving myself to choose
I decided to put my heart on a truce
Getting straight drunk on the Goose
Saw her name on my phone, pressed ignore
Heard a noise and went straight to the door
She walked in and ask why I played ghost
I told her that I couldn't be with her in fear
To bring someone that I may want to call dear
She said we don't have to get that close
Give me a swig of the Goose, (kiss the rose)
I said what do you really want from me?
She stripped down and said 'to be with me'

I sat back in my chair as she gave her body
She danced to our song before a sexy sesh
Loving her moves as we become one flesh
Later that night, I guess it was half a start
That we both gave each other half of our hearts

#43 Name Another Girl

The Declaration of Introduction:
You write that all girls are the same
You write that I'm the best in my skills
You even know my threats and my kills
I do everything that she can't do
You know that shit will always be true
So why do you even rock with her?
Why do you allow her to even shame me?
When I'm the one that you claim babe?
(She's) Ready, (I'm) Set, (Let's) Go!

Part One:
I'm the girl that you will always call a blessing
You bring in a girl that is (for your attention) possessing
Now you wonder why I am always stressing
If she doesn't ride you like I can,
Why do you fuck with her?
If she doesn't side with you like I can,
Why do you fuck with her?
All the shit she does will be temporary
When you and I are clearly legendary
Yet you say that bitch is true company
Making me feel like a second selection
Nigger answer the God-damn question!

Chorus:

Name another girl that will ride with you
Name another girl that will side with you
Name another girl that will multiply for you
Name another girl that will testify for you
Tell me boy, who will do it all?
I'm the one you can always call
Don't let that bitch make you fall

Part Two:

All those things that I did right
Turning nightmares into dreams
Yet, you call that bitch a delight
I'm so ready to cause a scene
Let me make myself very clear
I'll show a side that all men will fear
Proving them that I am not some game
Standing out of the fire, saying I have no shame
I'm not like those bitches you love on the pole
So, I'll sing it like my girl K. Cole
"Yeah Bitch, I'm Rick James"
Turning everything into complete shatter
Everything you say doesn't even matter

Chorus:

Name another girl that will ride with you
Name another girl that will side with you
Name another girl that will multiply for you
Name another girl that will testify for you
Tell me boy, who will do it all?
I'm the one you can always call
Don't let that bitch make you fall

Part Three:

Babe, I need you to choose me

I know that you don't want to lose me

I stood with you when you had nothing

(Doesn't that count for something?)

I'll be the one that will give you everything

(Doesn't that count for something?)

Even when you made me feel the worst,

I have always put you and only you first

I give it to you whenever you want it

That bitch will always see me as spiteful competition

Babe, don't make me fight for my rightful position

Chorus:

Name another girl that will ride with you

Name another girl that will side with you

Name another girl that will multiply for you

Name another girl that will testify for you

Tell me boy, who can do it all?

I'm the one you will always call

Don't let that bitch make you fall

#44 Ride with Me

Pre-Chorus:
(You should) ride with me, (you should) ride with me
That's what she said to me
(You should) ride with me, (you should) ride with me
That's what she said to me
Are you down to ride with me?

Part One:
I know that you are looking for a sexy queen
Not just a girl that can rock those sexy jeans
Show you things that you have never seen
All those others better know how to shut it
I can be that type of woman that can strut it
The drinks, the sex and all that you swim in
I am so much better than those other women
I can be that Heavenly and Earthly girl
Don't even rock with the flirty girl
Stick with me and we will always have the cream

Chorus:
(You should) ride with me, (you should) ride with me
That's what she said to me
(You should) ride with me, (you should) ride with me
That's what she said to me
Are you down to ride with me?

Part Two:

I can get all your engines roaring
Be the one that gets your heart soaring
Bet you that I won't make life boring
On my life, you'll be forever adoring
All those other bitches acted so fine
Thinking they were the top of the line
I can proudly laugh and say not this time
See, you need a real woman that can keep it fifty-fifty
Matter of fact, spilt it all down with me fifty-fifty
Even when you write about me in your testimony
You'll get the royalty and my deepest loyalty
I'm the girl that won't switch up and act so brand new
I'm the same girl that calls you when I'm in your avenue
I'm the same girl that has nerves of steels
Dangerous but sexy skills stunning in heels
So, sit back and relax as I'm burning the wheel
Turning this night into one hell of a deal

Chorus:

(You should) ride with me, (you should) ride with me
That's what she said to me
(You should) ride with me, (you should) ride with me
That's what she said to me
Are you down to ride with me?

#45 Getaway Sex/...Space Donut (Interlude)

Part One, Two, Three:
You love it when I smell like Sandalwood
You love it when we burn like candlewood
Contemplating on the The-Dream
Can we have Runaway Sex?
Producing on my story of a scene
Can we make some Getaway Sex?
This is what I mean...
When I'm with you, it's a vacation
Just cruising through with no destination
Sipping on some Malibu and Sprite
Just me and you as we call this right
As we toast on some Brandy,
Are you the Angel in Disguise?
As we drink on some brandy,
You make facials with surprises
Showing off your fine apple
Lips as fresh as pineapple
From the way you talk with beauty
The way we spark on some ecstasy
Kissing in the dark with chemistry
Do I call you an Art of Poetry?
Let me wrap my hands around your waist
As your panties hit the floor with desire
Grind slow and let's not ruin this in a haste
Creating colors in this heat of our fire
Hands on your body while sexing you all over

Swirling in the sheets, mixing on this sexy beat
Sex so good, I got you swept up off your feet
Without your love, I swear I will go nuts
Give me your love as I begin Space Donuts

#46 Space Donuts

Part One:
Say World, spare me on the memory
(Don't want to be caught up wilding out)
Say Girl, can you be my remedy?
(Sometimes it is better than crying out)
I don't want to float away in this race
When I look deep in your face
I want you to be better than ecstasy
You keep me so level in outer space
Sexing and smoking is how we communicate
If you promise me that sexy peach,
I can deliver on this sexy speech

Part Two:
Stay on top of me and dominant
As your beauty truly…illuminates
The pleasure of your sex is like pastries
You define the taste of sex so perfectly
The flavour of your femininity
Strawberry, blueberry, raspberries
One taste of both lips and I'm shook
Blackberry, black-cherry, wild berries
Running down like a babbling brook
Love, Sex, Passion and Temptation
This is the sweeter side of life we living in
Make this moment better than cinnamon

Part Three:

Let me make myself crystal clear
You take me to a new atmosphere
Making everything into yesteryears
You get me higher than some brownies
I don't need those other type of pastries
Since you are the one who is down for me
The sex is so good, I'll treat you in lace
Recklessly speaking, just stay on this flow
The sex is so good, I'll eat you in space
Recklessly speaking, just stay on this flow

#47 Recklessly Speaking

The Declaration of Introduction:
Recklessly Speaking,
Some can call this story boastful
I'm just living my life dangerously
Recklessly Speaking,
My true friends call me hopeful
When I can give it all away generously
Swear it on my life to the end
Welcome to my life my friends
Recklessly Speaking...
(She's) Ready, (I'm) Set, (Let's) Go!

Part One:
Recklessly Speaking,
How can you blame me for my taste in women?
Give me the mini flirts and give me the mini skirt
Recklessly Speaking,
How can you shame me for my chase of women?
Give me the full bottles and the full throttle
Speeding down the 101 singing 101
This is how we live under the sun
All around the world and you all shine like pearls
Slick talks to quick walks to set the mood
Wake up and can't name that face of the woman
Damn girl, don't you even judge me
When all of them want to hug me
Feeling breezy, they love me, they love me, they love me
The Women, Whisky and Symphony

I've sampled them all recklessly
While trying to keep up this memory
Aim to provide the sound of pleasure
Granting everything with a smile
Right down to your inner treasure
I'm the servant with a taste of style

Part Two:
Recklessly Speaking,
I am the guy that can do it all
Recklessly Speaking,
Buy out six or seven malls
This is a guy that knows how to ball
Be that guy that you can call
Don't count me out and let me fall
Since all your past ones were lame
I know I can bring them to shame
This isn't me trying to compensate
Just a man that can simply elevate
Drinking a flask in a shape of a fish
Ask for anything and I'll grant your wish
Slam dunk to your heart, call it swish swish
The Women, Whisky and Symphony
I've sampled them all recklessly
While trying to keep up this memory
Aim to provide the sound of pleasure
Granting everything with a smile
Right down to your inner treasure
I'm the servant with a taste of style

#48 The Flavour of Femininity (Bonus)

The Declaration of Introduction:
Recklessly Speaking, when was the last time I stopped and smelled your roses?
With your flavour of femininity,
You define that taste of sex so perfectly
Metaphorically speaking, when was the last time I stopped and got to know you?
Each woman has her own fragrance
Each feminine flavour is as unique and tasteful
Much to her plentiful personalities
Designed to lure and linger
From her seductress figure and face
Against my face you trace with your finger
Taking me back to a familiar place
(She's) Ready, (I'm) Set, (Let's) Go.

Part One:
You got my mind racing senseless
Driving fast on this burning swerve
You're leaving me so breathless
Starting at your silhouette as you undress
As the raindrops sparkle in the wind
Releasing your sweet aroma
Fresh air after a thunderstorm
So softly subtly spoken words

When you take me down to the floor,
Leaving me breathing for more
Swear to God, you will never be a bore
Give me one more round, call it an encore

Part Two:
Your appearance is a showstopper
Something bigger than a movie star
Caking is what you truly are
Something as sweet as a vanilla bean
Without your essence, I'll turn to a hella fiend
A man can't focus without a woman's scent
So, I'll spend for it down to the very last cent
Let's make this sexy moment some kind of ruse
She checks me and I check her
When we intertwine, It's a muse
We Sixty-Nine style for the nectar
On my life, you keep getting better
Steamy moments to break the sweat
We don't even need to take a rest
You're acing my heart like a test

Part Three:
Saturate the air to flutter this heart
The fragrance of your body as a start
I'm cuddling you tight to not be apart
My body completely heavy and relaxed
You are taking over this muse
I'm savoring every minute of you
I just want to taste your inner flavor
I want to drink you down with no chaser

Strawberry, blueberry, raspberries
One taste of your lips and I'm shook
Blackberry, black-cherry, wild berries
Running down like a babbling brook
When we go on a level so intelligently
Savoring your mind as sapiosexuality
Release your Flavour of Femininity
Creating a flavour just for me only
I sign off this poem successfully

#49 Heat of Passion

Part One:
Babe, do you even need an excuse?
From the way that you seduce?
Trailing a fresh line of your perfume
Your love is all that I want to consume
You turn this moment into a non-fiction
Those Rainy/Days always got you wet
You turn this moment into a fun tradition
Smiling on the first day that we met
So many ways to make you sweat
We rough sex to ease the tension
We burn hard to create the affection
We go deep to reach the ascension
I say your body is of high demand
Your legs, I want you to spread it
As if you got some contraband
The things we do in this bed (shit)
Only the walls will understand

Chorus:
In the heat of passion
The world slips away
In the heat of passion
Let's stay in bed today
In the heat of passion
This girl is down to play
In the heat of passion

Part Two:

When you walk into the room naked,
It's getting hard to bite my tongue
High heels, hair down, I can't take it
Can we go and right this wrong?
Painting chocolate down your spine
Man, you really are a work of art
You know how to keep me in line
Drinking red wine with you as mine
Your red lips took me on a head trip
Teasing and pleasing until I drip
I eat your cherry like a banquet
Licking it to change the language
I treat your body like a blanket
Wrapping it in kisses and compliments

Chorus:

In the heat of passion
The world slips away
In the heat of passion
Let's stay in bed today
In the heat of passion
This girl is down to play
In the heat of passion

Part Three:

There is a certain heat of passion
Igniting flames in this sensual haze
When our bodies spark on reaction
We can roll up on this natural blaze
I own many treasures from the start
I give it all away, so we won't be apart

You're pouring pleasure in my heart
But first, do that walk as you strip down
So, we can talk with just our lips now
I love it when we show our true skin
Our true desire is revealed as a sin?
Damn girl…we really should give in
To something we've never felt before
Your kisses make me melt and more
You got me grinning so mischievously
Believing that this must be serendipity
Devilishly smiling on the likes of you
Playfully taking two or more bites of you
Taking you down so mercilessly
Going in circles in the sign of infinity
Strawberry, blueberry, raspberries
Tasting your true Flavour of Femininity

Chorus:
In the heat of passion
The world slips away
In the heat of passion
Let's stay in bed today
In the heat of passion
This girl is down to play
In the heat of passion

#50 Reckless Knockout (Conclusion)

The Declaration of Destruction:

Recklessly Speaking,

Everyone has a past

Good, bad, or indifferent

We shared some laugh, shared some tears

That's what being a good girlfriend is

Recklessly Speaking,

Everyone has a past

Good, bad, or indifference

We shared some laughs, shared some fears

That's what being a good boyfriend is

Yet, we can't say we both did that

Recklessly Speaking,

Running low on this whisky and this memory

She said to tell this story truthfully and soberly

This could be the last time to tell you all the truth

(She's) Ready to attack, (I'm) Set to do the same, (Let's) Go ignite this final fight.

Part One:

I'm not trying to start this argument (now)

But seeing you hurt is punishment (wow)

She said choose your words carefully

What one woman won't do, another woman will

Is that where you stand?

She said choose your words carefully
What one man won't do, another man will
Is that where you stand?
She said choose your words carefully
You say you love me, and you put it on everything
But now, those words seem to sound like nothing
Right now, I don't care anymore
We can't even see eye to eye
I'm ready to leave and say goodbye
Spare me the pain, the rain, the tears and swear
Do that shit all in my face and I won't even care
You and I can't even be equal
So, don't even ask for us to be a sequel

Part Two:
As my love for you is becoming sparingly
I'm going to make this next point quickly
Why can't you do anything without a drink?
Why don't you even want to stop and think?
Look at life and just brush it off with a wink?
When reality returns to you in a crash
You'll just do all this shit again in a dash
All those bitches can't fill that hole
The ones you really wanted to smash
All those bitches can't make you whole
All the whisky can't make you sane
All the music can't erase the pain
You don't want to listen to reason
Yet, you know I'm telling the truth
I call out against you like treason
Don't even try to play the good guy
I'm ready to leave and say goodbye
Spare me the pain, the rain, the tears and swear

Do that shit all in my face and I won't even care
You and I can't even be equal
So, don't even ask for us to be a sequel

Part Three:
I'll come against you with all my artillery
Rain down bullets until you understand
Tell you those were just warning shots
Falling into madness is the final straw
Until I redefine the word traumatic
I'll bust out the automatic
For the shit you've done so wrong
I have taken it for so long
Unlike you, I'll fight for us to make it work for this
Leave those bitches that can only twerk for it
On your life, heavy drinking is not attractive
You only have one life to give
Remember I said I love you first
But if you want to go, then you are the worst
I'm ready to leave and say goodbye
Spare me the pain, the rain, the tears and swear
Do that shit all in my face and I won't even care
You and I can't even be equal
So, don't even ask for us to be a sequel

THE SECOND DECLARATION OF DEDICATION:

Moonlight of Seduction

(Part One)

I'm often known to speaking in codes,

Mixing the truth and some fantasies

Down this life filled with bumpy roads

Moments where I did and didn't blow it

At the end of all these testimonies

Hoping that you will see through it

It's time to tell you the Second part of the truth...

Welcome to The Five Suns of Amatory II: Moonlight of Seduction (Part One)

The (Poetic) Introduction: Hopeless Romantic (Intro-lude)

Part One, Two, Three:

You Hopeless Romantic

I know that you won't quit

Every time you start your script

Keep on writing to ease into the flow

You Hopeless Romantic,

Every time you start your script

I know that you are thinking about me

I know that you are drinking about me

I know when you are praying for me

Face the music, I'm much more than therapeutic

In your erotic tales

That sweet serene of your true feelings of devotion

There I am glowing from your confession

Writing the loneliness off the pages of adoration

If words fail to portray,

You will always have this way

This is my chapter promise to you

Your actions speak much volume on you

There we can echo the next line in two…

I want you

I need you

I love you…

We all have forbidden clandestine (of Sex and Desire)

Exchange them with me in this second book

Sing to me my sweet Valentine (of Sex and Desire)

Don't give those other bitches a second look

Come and roll with me on this Vegas Dice

I can make your life greater than paradise

Let me do what I am notorious for…

Creating everything with a melody

Killing everything that is deadly

Erasing everything that is heavy

I'm just a taste of curiosity

Until you go deeper…

Then you call me familiarity

                Once a house now turned into a home

I promise to never make you feel alone

For the woman you merit

I can designate every flavour,

For the woman who will get it,

Hope they serve and I cater

My venomous desires are sharper, sexier and faster

Your love for me is as safe as being in a sanctuary

Then those other bitches, you will wave 'see you later'

Welcome to the Second Session of the Suns of Amatory

#51 Rainy/Days (Cabin)

Part One:
Recklessly Speaking,
I know that you have that cabin so exclusive
Recklessly Speaking,
I know that you will wear satin that will be explosive
Taking selfies in bed in the morning
I love your style in a Black Cammie
Not missing a beat on everything
I love your smile in a Black Cammie
Playing some Nineties Throwback
Sing it loud, we got one life to live
Specifically, on some R&B Throwback
On some deep Sexual Healing
Your sultry ways got me jonesing
I'm talking about you in terms of boasting
Without your love, I'm bugging

Part Two:
Recklessly Speaking, what if we could disappear?
Recklessly Speaking, let me make myself clear
From the very first moment that we met
When you invited me to go this weekend
To the cabin that's as upscale as Manhattan
Transformed it to a night of passion
I can't reveal who you are yet
It's been a whirlwind of questions
Taking me to a place of seclusion
Posing yourself of mere perfection

Good girl, Bad girl, such an illusion
Split/Second thinking with no conclusion
Messing me up like a psychedelic drug
Pulling me closer like a magnetic hug
Your seductive words rain in my ear
That rainy day that took all weekend
You're bringing up steamy memories
Go slow as I start up the romance
You're melting in your silky panties
Go low as we touch and dance
Let's not make this moment hazy
Can we do a little *Sumthin' Sumthin'*?
Without you, I swear I'll go crazy

#52 Gossip

Part One:

Temptation always got me in a toss up
Adoration talks about you like gossip
Going back and forth on this blend of truth
Wait, I'm tripping on a friend name Ruth
One sees you as a goddess girl
While one paints you as the hottest girl
I just want you to come closer
Start off by kissing your shoulder
Reflecting for a Spilt/Second on you
When you stayed for some breakfast
Walking in your lacy black panties on
You love it when we can be so reckless
Sexing without your black panties on
Turning down all of the commotion
Making love while going in motion
Burning down all of our emotion
Sweating and swearing to submission
Words exchanged in the deepest passion
Can we keep going with this action?

Part Two:

Temptation always got me in a toss up
Adoration talks about you like gossip
They have no reason to lie to me
Making you the true talk in society
When they call you that girl of variety.
Getting my head in your space now

Making you cum as you please
While I'm tasting you in a face down
Making you cum as you please
To break the cycle of this tease
From the bed, the car, to the bar
Seeing where we can take it this far
Starting with your number and name
Babe, I'm not playing any games
Take a chance on me with no shame
So that you and I can go forward,
Read this second part backward

Part Three:
Temptation always got me in a toss up
Adoration talks about you like gossip
Your love got me feeling hyperactive
You got me so deep in your vibes
You are that girl that is so attractive
Describing all your features and quality
This story is getting better and better
Nodding on your speakers and harmony
This is a moment that's worth to remember
Love when you tease with your body
Shorty, I love it when you are horny
Kissing me down on the counter
Carrying you up to the shower
Slip and sliding for an hour
Simply blooming in your flower
Moving towards the bedroom with your direction
Providing you that tease and desire
Doing all those freaky positions with no hesitation
Until you and I both come from this cease-fire

#53 Sharing Some Tunes

Part One:

Before this song is over,

Can we be shadows in the park?

First, we exchange some tunes this time

Then we can disappear in this music

Staring at the skyscraper and stars so therapeutic

We on this magnitude of this reality

From the attitudes of our chemistry

Twisting coincidence and sultry

Making you and me so certainly

I like the way you move on this beat

Floating around in this wonderland

Sparking me like a catalyst

Booming loud in this jungle land

Tell me girl, are you a hypnotist?

I like the way you take me off my feet

We can create some magic in this heat

We can make so much composition

To beat our heaters and competitions

Chorus:

So can I stay up all night with you?

Just sharing and exchanging some tune?

So can I stay up all night with you?

Just sharing and exchanging some tune?

So can I stay up all night with you?

Part Two:

Before this song is over,

Can we be shadows in the park?

We're held in the rhythm of the sleep

Soaring comets after comets on this tune

This is my chapter promise to you

Don't close your eyes on this scene

Stay awake with me in this dream

Can you feel the rhythm in your soul?

The heavy medley of the city playing tonight

Sexy saxophones and trumpets

Smoothly plays as we exchange flights

Sexy pianos and violins so clear

You got your own beat right here

Up in the air as we lay on the ground

I want to know all your sounds

Chorus:

So can I stay up all night with you?

Just sharing and exchanging some tune?

So can I stay up all night with you?

Just sharing and exchanging some tune?

So can I stay up all night with you?

Part Three:

Before this song is over,

Will you play me your melody?

Before this song is over,

Will you come and rescue me?

Before this song is over,

Will you partake in this dance with me?

Before this song is over,

Will you take this chance with me?

#54 Satin and Soul

Part One:
How would you feel if we did this in reverse?
I got something that we can do tonight
Get on this wave train of poetry
I'll run you a bath filled with champagne and honey
Bubbles trapping your troubles
Up in the air as you pop them gone
As you crave something long
I'll just give it to you in this song
I'll feed you some berries (for pleasure)
I'll kiss you merrily (to feel like forever)
Sexing you well in awe and admiration
Simply giving you the right reaction
On touching your Satin and Soul
To continue this type of satisfaction
It's such a symphony for this soul

Part Two:
How would you feel if we did this in reverse?
I got something that we can do tonight
I'll drop my clothes to the ground
As you give me your heated gaze
Trust, I won't even make a sound
For this moment, I want to save
Your radiance in the light of the moon
My pupils wide open from your perfume
To your bra and panties, so fancy
Getting lost in between your thighs

Come close to me and get handy
Tongue swirls there to get you high
That panting and sweating kind of seduction
Escaping this world of corruption
To the point of this sultry salvation
Recklessly Speaking, I love you so much on this sex drive
Recklessly sexing with no interruption
When your body gets me on an automatic drive
We created earth shaking orgasms as a category five
After I get this chapter down on lock
Let's go and make an aftershock

Part Three:
How would you feel if we did this reverse?
I got something that we can do tonight
Before we go and just reminisce
You and I should share a soul kiss
Cause we can't go backwards on this Swoon
Let's play some Claire de Lune
Let's go forward to eating some macarons
While candles are lit around your room
Simply giving you the right reaction
On touching your satin and soul
To continue this type of satisfaction
It's such a symphony for this soul
Conversation deeper than an abyss
I love it when you act so flirty
Temptation stronger than any kiss
I love it when you act so dirty
Demanding that I go deeper and deeper
Until my heart said to keep her

#55 If God was a Bartender

The Declaration of Introduction:
I used to think that I got my life together
Show you my plans on graph paper
I used to think I got my life forever
Guess even you need a laugh ever now or later
For you got plans I don't understand (yet)
All I'm asking is a helping hand (bet)
But life shot me down and now it feels so messed up
It's getting late tonight, should I go and get fucked up?
Nah man. I should be getting home to nothing new
I'm not thinking straight tonight, why should I continue?
Old souls say I'm not alone in that department
They said have a drink and try to stay
Damn, That's some tough love compliment
A man walked toward me with no delay
He smiled and told me to try and pray
(God's) Listening, (I'm) Praying, (Let's) Go

Part One:
Life feels like a heavy burden
And I'm not trying to frame you
Life feels like a heavy burden
And I'm not trying to blame you
Sorry God, Forgive me for this shit
You made me and I can't take it
From my family to my friends
Feels like a loop that never ends
To my S/O that often feels like a no-show

I want to hold on when she often thinks of letting go
Can't be with me and it's killing my last sense to not be with her
What was the point to bless me with her when I can't be with her?
I'm not trying to challenge your storyline on her and me
But why won't you let us just be?
Please don't take her away no matter the lack of support
Please don't take me away as you are my last support

Chorus:
God, if you were like a Bartender,
Please serve me up some wisdom
God, if you were like a Bartender,
Please serve me up some wisdom,
Life may deal me some bad cards
But you on my side, it won't be hard
God, if you were like a Bartender,
Please serve me up some wisdom

Part Two:
I'm sorry that I'm not letting you talk by my side
I know that you have other patrons
In the end, I just want you to walk by my side
Changing my mind when I think of humanity with hatred
Simply remembering to love the ones that you've created
Let us have a moment, come on
I need to go on and vent
I really don't tell anyone to get bent
I don't want to get in the way of your infinite ways
But Dear God, I get the song by Hunter Hays
And I know that you don't mess up
But only you, I just want to fess up
I don't want to go into therapy

The walk of life is draining me
Please understand and carry me

Chorus:
God, if you were a like Bartender,
Please serve me up some wisdom
God, if you were a like Bartender,
Please serve me up some wisdom,
Life may deal me some bad cards
But you on my side, it won't be hard
God, if you were like a Bartender,
Please serve me up some wisdom

Part Three:
I can't look at life and act so tough
You know my heart has had enough
Serve me up a drink as you give me
The wisdom to cure the pain in me
Cutting me off for a minute on the alcohol
Ringing the bell saying last call, last call
You tell me that you will be with me not just for the night
You tell me that everything will be alright
Pain goes in this life to overcome the adversary
To give your life purpose and make it legendary
My creations say that I have not gone through it
This life, I have done the walk so they can't talk
Of the sorrows so that I will give them a tomorrow
From time to time, you will feel some joy and pain,
But everything under me, I want to give you to gain
After that, he poured me up and said be at peace

Chorus:

God, if you were like a Bartender,
Please serve me up some wisdom
God, if you were like a Bartender,
Please serve me up some wisdom,
Life may deal me some bad cards
But you on my side, it won't be hard
God, if you were like a Bartender,
Please serve me up some wisdom

#56 Cloud Nine (Poetic Interlude)

Part One:

All the days that I think about you
I thank God that you are real and true
I wouldn't know what I would do without you
So glad that you are finally mine
To love you, to hug you, to kiss you
To even miss you
Never felt like this before in authenticity
Cause with you, everything is so heavenly
As if I'm on Cloud Nine,
I'm ready to cross the line
You speed through my head like a train
Ripping the cloud and bringing in the rain
Shower your appreciation on me
All before you told me your name
And I would do the very same

Part Two:

You're the one that keeps life exciting
You're the one that keeps me writing
You're the one that has love and lust combining
You're the one that keeps me ruminating
On love that I was hoping and praying
I just want you all to myself
Cause you are my Cloud Nine
I want you all the time
When we touch and kiss
I want you all the time
You always keep me grinning

I want you all the time
As we keep on living

Part Three:
Normally, I would write about any girl like a wish list
Hoping that I would get all that I asked for,
Now for the first time, I don't need to do this shit
About sex and love, you finally got me preach-less
For the first time, you left me speechless
For the first time, I can't write about you anymore
Because God stepped in and gave me the unexpected
He gave me something better than my letters
He finally gave me you in the flesh
You became as real as real can be
Love said that you are the one for me
As we enter Cloud Nine,
Will you partake on some dark wine?

#57 Cloud Nine (The Testimony)

Part One:

Babe, you are my Xscape
The Softest Place on Earth
Babe, you are my Xscape
The Softest Place on Earth
Matter of Fact, you are my Heaven on Earth
I love you and the curves of you
You are my sun and my sky
You are my fresh oxygen
and my best friend
I don't want to swerve from you
So, let's run and hide
To a place where love is like breathing
Since you in my life has a new meaning
On my life, I'll never consider cheating
Cause Babe girl, you give me that feeling

Chorus:

As we go into Cloud Nine
You got me leaning so high
As we go into Cloud Nine
I'm breathing you with a sigh
Entering your world so divine
Let's just bounce on this flow
As we go into Cloud Nine
Go on and run this show

Part Two:

I love it when you make that sound

Something like singing angels

I love it when you say you will stay around

Because you got me believing in being faithful

I'm your King and you are my Queen

I'll give you things that you haven't seen

Medium High cause we're smoking loudly

Walking in the park when it's getting cloudy

Comedian vibes cause we're joking proudly

Cruising in the dark, Shining in my Audi

You are everything that I ever want in a woman

Let's celebrate you like it's Christmas

I'll sing the next line better than the musician Avant

Your Body is the Business

Never in my life would I want you as a mistress

As I got that one special girl that is forever my Mistress

Chorus:

As we go into Cloud Nine

You got me leaning so high

As we go into Cloud Nine

I'm breathing you with a sigh

Entering your world so divine

Let's just bounce on this flow

As we go into Cloud Nine

Go on and run this show

#58 Something New

The Declaration of Introduction:
Like a shooting star, I saw something beautiful leaving so soon
From the cloudy skies of a summertime evening kind of swoon
An angelic figure in the flesh
One word and she made it all calm
Turning my life into a success
Hitting that button of life to a rest
Changing my life for the better
Can you and I please go together?
Even if you and I weren't written to be forever?
(She's) Ready, (I'm) Set, (Let's) Go

Part One:
Life is unexplainable when we walk individually
Until I met you and you said I made you happy
Time is expandable when it's with you only
Life is manageable when you hold me
Living in this world of imagination
Toasting it up as if we are in a celebration
You are my best girl; my motivation
Living my life, your life to new destination
Travel around the world about five times
I'll cheer your name like it's prime time
You get my head straight when I'm out of line
Getting all caught up and getting my shit together
You get my head straight when I'm out of line
Getting all caught up and getting my shit together

Chorus:

Every time I want to do something new, I want to do it with you

You share your life and I will share mine

Every time I want to do something new, I want to do it with you

You share your life and I will share mine

Every time I want to do something new, I want to do it with you

Part Two:

You give that one up

When the sun is up

It's a brand-new day

To life, I can go all the way

A new life, a new wave starts

Against these bitches, you got the brave heart

When the sun is down.

Can we have some fun right now?

On some fancy drinks and silly banter

I can go all night with you

On some curly fries and fancy wine

I can go all night with you

Trying new things with some laughs

Letting the good time strolling in

Babe, you and me is a win

Without you in my life, consider it a sin

You get my head straight when I'm out of line

Getting all caught up and getting my shit together

You get my head straight when I'm out of line

Getting all caught up and getting my shit together

Chorus:

Every time I want to do something new, I want to do it with you

You share your life and I will share mine

Every time I want to do something new, I want to do it with you

You share your life and I will share mine

Every time I want to do something new, I want to do it with you

#59 The Breakup Testimony Finale: EXit Dream

Previously on The Breakup Testimony... (Go back to #26)

The Declaration of Introduction/Chorus:

My head is on my X

I'm not thinking the best

My head is on my X

Is this some kind of test?

I thought I could put this to bed

But now you got back in my head

I promised that this will not be a loop

From everything that you have read

For the very last time, here is the scoop

(She's) been over Me, (I'm) Swearing it's the last time, (Let's) just let her Go

Part One:

I know that you have set your ways

About us you stop reminiscing now

You and me should just stay away

But against my heart, I'm not listening now

Yes, it hurts that you won't forgive me

You have every right not to

But I pray that isn't true

All this time and you wrote me out your life

Now you look at me as the deceiver

Was I really that bad of a guy to give you that strife?

This is my last chance to make you a believer

All I'm asking for you is a successful Recovery

I (used to) pray for us at night
One last attempt…alright?
But before I lose you on this beat
I'll do anything to make your heart beat
Just listen to me on this repeat

Chorus:
My head is on my X
I'm not thinking the best
My head is on my X
Is this some kind of test?
I thought I could put this to bed
But now you got back in my head
I promised that this will not be a loop
From everything that you have read
For the very last time, here is the scoop

Part Two:
There's a Pain in my Heart,
So let's Smoke, Drink, Break Up
Bumping and drinking on some Mila J.
While doing some shots of Tequila (hey)
Marshall headphone on to tune you out
Musiq said It Is what It Is… (Repeat on)
That song is us now… don't even pout
Whenever my heart goes dear… (Beats on)
My friends in high places tell me to let you go
All that negative energy when you look at me
It is the only thing *you* hold on as a memory
I don't want to remember you and me like that

No bad blood, but I'm poison on
You not wanting to try again
Start over and be friends again
You were the girl I wanted in my life
As you once dreamt that we would
Be husband and wife
But I guess you say that was some ages ago
Something like the stories I wrote some pages ago
One Night in the Park…
Guess there's no more of that talk
Drawing up a memory from this pencil line
Do you remember our time in Kensal Rise?
It was a second escape for me
Even after what we used to be
But before I lose you on this beat
I'll do anything to make your heart beat
Just listen to me on this repeat

Chorus:
My head is on my X
I'm not thinking the best
My head is on my X
Is this some kind of test?
I thought I could put this to bed
But now you got back in my head
I promised that this will not be a loop
From everything that you have read
For the very last time, here is the scoop

Part Three:

As I make this close on this turn,
One day I hope you give a second chance
But you want these roses to burn
What stays in the past, stays in the past
But I want you in my life as a romance
But you still think of me as indigestion
Then answer this final question
Will you one day forgive me?
To go and grant me that peace?
Or would you rather have me deceased?
You say that people will never change
I found that remotely strange
So, what do you call a reborn sinner?
I considered them reborn winners
All I'm asking is for an honest reset
But before I lose you on this beat
I'll do anything to make your heart beat
Just listen to me on this repeat

Chorus:

My head is on my X
I'm not thinking the best
My head is on my X
Is this some kind of test?
I thought I could put this to bed
But now you got back in my head
I promised that this will not be a loop
From everything that you have read
For the very last time, here is the scoop

#60 The Lingering Smoke of Midnight

Part One:
Woke up in the bright light city
Filled with the glitter, girls, and a guitar
Last night felt like a mystery
Songs that linger like a smoke on a cigar
Flashing the red and blue lights
Racing down in my getaway car
Dashing feds as we took flight
Soaring straight into the sky
Seeing things in such a haze
Rolling it and let's start a blaze
Blowing it all like its cosmic dust
Going into space from this supply
Reviving my words from this Poetic Rust

Part Two:
Resting on the fresh cut lawn
In this cloud covering the city
Smoking Midnight till the break of dawn
Last night felt like a mystery
But I'm still on some query
Filled with no regret or affair
Woke up with some morning Hennessey
One hand holding your underwear
Let the vapor of memories ignite
Lingering from our sexual chemistry
You're swimming in a pool of rosé
After taking off your finest lingerie
I dive in after you before the sunrise

Until both spirits are ready to face time
Drown me in the taste of that sweet wine

Part Three:
Pull me down as I take my last breath
Exotic kisses are considered the best
From this, I'll be drunk to death
Erotic kisses are considered the best
Reviving me from the bitter test
Return to the surface soaking in drinks
Laying on the blanket as I think
You all in my head, I need a shrink
To tell of the crazy things we should do
Blowing smoke from the e-cig called BLU
Make it come to life and for us to be true

#61 Beyond the Night (Part Two): Acceleration

The Declaration of Introduction:

Last time I nearly see my demise
That was not a near miss
But you gave me another chance to revise
Back to life from your kiss
As you offer something new
This could be so dangerous
As you obtain this new drug
Are you not a bit curious?
This will be better than a hug
Please don't be so serious
Just try this new prescription
With a twist called Acceleration
(She's) Ready, (I'm) Set, (Let's) Go

Part One:

Off the west coast, we're driving this blue convertible
From a story about 29 miles ago that was almost true
Surviving the head rush that was manageable
Why does it always have to be about you?
She acquires a new taste in the light
As she turns into my healer
She acquires a new chase for the night
As she turns into my dealer
Hallucinations with no destination
She feels me and I feel her
As she proposes a new proposition
To release our imagination

Escape life as a cut, copy and paste
She gave me one to try as a taste
Everything moving in a fast pace
What do you have me on?
What is happening to my last face?
What do you have me on?
The light is quickly disappeared in fright
Everything is getting clearer in this night
Shooting stars over the horizon
Moving in a New York Minute times two
Sipping on this right hope (Whisky)
Walking on this tight rope (Trust me)

Part Two:
Is it wrong that I don't want to stop?
You double our prescription
Is it wrong that I don't want to stop?
Take a pause on this intermission
This is the moment I've chosen
This mind's faster than Sonic
This subscription made us frozen
Ain't this some shit?
Same story, different chapter
Feeling higher than paradise
Same story, different chapter
Skating in this moment on ice
It was so worth taking this twice

Part Three:
Now it's getting dangerous
You want to triple our subscription
You still being ever so generous

From the start of the introduction

Swimming inside the memories

Creating us brand new identities

To enter realms with no hesitation

Now we are feeling better than a gold rush

We took it and felt the triple effect

Without considering the complication

Since the dose was too much

Negative vibes created a ripple effect

Turning to a struggle for us not to knock out

As one of us just went into a full knock out

Part Four:

The heart is beating fast

But its retreating slowly

The heart is beating fast

But its retreating slowly

My body is starting to go

The Acceleration as it turns out

This shit will eventually burn out

Was it worth this risk?

She must watch me on my last breath

Was it worth this risk?

Her Kiss of Life is considered death

As I laugh, I'm not quitting

This stuff was worth the ride

She smiles; you are winning

So, come lay right by my side

Tell the people that I will be alright

I finally reached Beyond the Night

#62 Trailblazer

Part One:

She's drawn so perfectly from my sketches
And yet...She's the one that broke out the trenches
She walks out of the page of passion
When she rewrote the meaning of beauty and ecstasy
Wearing satin to capture the weak in desire
Strutting down through the streaks of fire
Let the flames show your true face
You stand before everyone with grace
Creating everything with a melody
Killing everything that is deadly
Erasing everything that is heavy

Part Two:

Now that you got my attention
Let me say that you are a woman of perfection
All those other girls were such a delight
Now here you are being my only appetite
Why should we even deny it?
Don't even try and hide it
You are the woman that can buy it
Sail around the world like a pirate
Creating everything with a melody
Killing everything that is deadly
Erasing everything that is heavy

Part Three:

As I stand and applaud you girl

Go on and create your empire

As I stand and applaud you girl

Through the fire, you will go higher

As I stand and applaud you girl

Be the Queen and I'm your sire

So sexy, smooth and beautiful

Having you in my life is unforgettable

Give you these last lines so memorable

Creating everything with a melody

Killing everything that is deadly

Erasing everything that is heavy

#63 Saké Lovers I & II: K-Pop and Chill

Part One:

I'm curious,

Our friendship needs a pause

I'm serious,

Our friendship actually has a clause

As we both said we had a fantasy

Something like a sexy fire

But we kept it glowing in memory

Time to leave this friend zone

We can first start off to chill

To work us up to this thrill

Maybe we can do what we do again

Pour us a cup of premium Saké

As you leave to sip into something comfy

Mind going dark now, way to numb me

Chorus:

Babe, don't you stop

(As we chill on some K-Pop,

chill on some K-Pop, chill on some K-Pop)

Babe, don't you stop

(As we chill on some K-Pop,

chill on some K-Pop, chill on some K-Pop)

Babe, don't you stop

(As we chill on some K-Pop,

chill on some K-Pop, chill on some K-Pop)

Part Two:

You walked out of your room and got me in a stun

Damn it, You Don't Play Fair

I know tonight we are going to have some fun

Stunning in your underwear

Sexy, are you ready for this play?

Let's lay on the floor to feel the mood

The drinks are coming in like a full tide

Let's play some K-Pop to start this ride

I'm looking at you in a brand new view

Doing some freaky thing to you

I want to flip you open like a garage

When you said that you want a massage

Give you a kiss that will ignite you

Feel on your booty to excite you

Strip you down to see your breasts

Pulling your hair to claim dominance

Pressed gently against my chest

Establishing my sex as prominence

Taking you down to the floor

Hope this is going right

Get your mind on this tour

As we go deep in the night

Chorus:

Babe, don't you stop

(As we chill on some K-Pop,

chill on some K-Pop, chill on some K-Pop)

Babe, don't you stop

(As we chill on some K-Pop,

chill on some K-Pop, chill on some K-Pop)

Babe, don't you stop
(As we chill on some K-Pop,
chill on some K-Pop, chill on some K-Pop)

Part Three:
I'm not even going to lie
We need to set the mood
Damn, you look so fly
Cooking us some food
Serving me steak and whisky
You got me feeling so frisky
Share a glass with me
I'll pour you some Sake
So you can ease in and rock me
I'll undress you from this locket
I'll feed you some Godiva chocolate
I know that you want to do some BDSM
So we can do it every now and again
Make it a night that I won't forget
Wake up to you with no regrets

Chorus:
Babe, don't you stop
(As we chill on some K-Pop,
chill on some K-Pop, chill on some K-Pop)
Babe, don't you stop
(As we chill on some K-Pop,
chill on some K-Pop, chill on some K-Pop)
Babe, don't you stop
(As we chill on some K-Pop,
chill on some K-Pop, chill on some K-Pop)

#64 Saké Lover III: Kiss & Run

Part One:

As I sat next to you on the train
I didn't expect it to be a reality
All we did was being cheeky
I thought after we shared an evening
When we combine good wine and some time
There were some words we said that's too revealing
Shared our first kiss in the elevator
Making it hotter than a radiator
Gave it more than a swirl
You like it when I bite your tongue
Damn, you got my mind sprung
Yes, I'm talking about you girl
But I have to snap back on the train
As we got out and walked in the rain

Chorus:

All we did was kiss
And you wanted to run
All we did was kiss
And you wanted to run
Even if we didn't cross the line
Let's not even waste no time
Even if all we did was kiss
And you wanted to run

Part Two:
Because I knew this might be a one off
I wanted to keep kissing you
Maybe becoming friends with benefits
You said you didn't feel the connection
So we stopped so we wouldn't be a write off
I shouldn't take it as a rejection
No emotional attachment for the hell of it
Since our kiss was somewhat close to perfection
I'm just saying we both on this notion,
This is how I feel
If you don't want a part of me,
It's no big deal
When you said that's it's on you
For that, I can't be mad at you
But I have to snap back on the train
As we got out and walked in the rain

Chorus:
All we did was kiss
And you wanted to run
All we did was kiss
And you wanted to run
Even if we didn't cross the line
Let's not even waste no time
Even if all we did was kiss
And you wanted to run

Part Three:
We can still stay and be friends
Toast it up to us on the clink
We can still stay and be friends

No blame on us or the drinks

Just airing us out on this poetry

Since that kiss became the remedy

For us to do what we want in this fantasy

Open up on this idea to be friendly

And maybe if we had one too many

Then we can cross it again in reality

Contemplating on us on some fun

Do it on the low in your home

Grab the condoms and shut down our phones

Strip you out of your wet jeans

So we can create this best scene

But I have to snap back on the train

As we got out and walked in the rain

Chorus:

All we did was kiss

And you wanted to run

All we did was kiss

And you wanted to run

Even if we didn't cross the line

Let's not even waste no time

Even if all we did was kiss

And you wanted to run

#65 Sipping on Some Heartbreak

The Declaration of Introduction:
She said what is the point of a heart if it keeps breaking?
I said that love is something that's worth the risk taking?
She said her heart is tired of being broken
She cried I truly feel like a wasted token
I said I know the feeling too recently
All of this pain will go away slowly
She said what was the drink in my hand?
I told her in exchange for the drink, she listens to my tale
With one kiss on the cheek and a swipe, she said start your tale
(She's) Ready, (I'm) Set, (Let's) Go.

Part One:
Don't flash your name on my phone
As you leave me with some dismay
Let your shame fall as I am alone
Thinking of you like I'm on a relay
As you leave me with some betray
(Wait a minute…shit).
Tears running down my face
We once had some spark
Telling me I'm not worth the chase
Now we both gone dark
I was the man in those songs
I don't see what went wrong

Now you say that you want to quit
Those words made my heart break
Losing me as if you don't give a shit
Fainting hard before starting to shake

Repeat:
Because of your selfish heart,
I'm sipping on some heartbreak
Because of your selfish heart
I'm sipping on some heartbreak
Because of your selfish heart
I'm sipping on some heartbreak

Part Two:
When did you become such a savage?
I can't take this pain anymore
I was the man that was well above average
There was a knock at the door
My heart instantly made a switch
Only seeing you as that bitch
Storming in my place as we began to fight
About our relationship to the stuff I brought
Hiding your fears knowing that you got caught
Lying that you were out with your girlfriends
Seeing that bastard made my whole world end
On that night, I actually saw you and I
Let Eros go on a fire squad until I (died)
All because you were the one that (lied)

Chorus:

Because of your selfish heart,
I'm sipping on some heartbreak
Because of your selfish heart
I'm sipping on some heartbreak
Because of your selfish heart
I'm sipping on some heartbreak

Part Three:

Why did you do it for so long?
As you said let me explain
Did I really do you so wrong?
I said, haven't you caused enough pain?
You say is our relationship worth the salvage
I say I was the man that was well above average
To you, I no longer want to be rude.
But to you and I, we have to conclude
We only have one life to live
So, I say no strife and only forgive
My heart and head both say be gone
Before you become that bitch in this song
I'll survive as I go through this weather so grey
Taking a new woman that will be down to play

Chorus:

Because of your selfish heart,
I'm sipping on some heartbreak
Because of your selfish heart
I'm sipping on some heartbreak
Because of your selfish heart
I'm sipping on some heartbreak

#66 Double Shot of Pineapples

Part One:
Travel the world with me like Prodigy
While we bop to the song of No Diggy
As you cheer to life and say Ready? Okay!
For your feelings, yes, I'm down to play
And in return, yes, I'm willing to stay
Read this next part like a headline
My sex drive for you is better than a vampire
Up all night as if I can sleep or expire
Running to see you before your deadline
Wake up with you and say that I got to kiss you
Even got you to say when I leave, you miss me

Part Two:
You'll spend so much on V.S, it will turn to black
Against these other girls, you wear it the best
Outfit so good, you rewrote my story of Sex Attack
That's the part, I'm deeply impressed
Please don't bring another man back to your home
Those other players will make you groan
I'm the best guy around when you are alone
Text me cheeky messages from your phone
I'll come over and make you moan
Kisses and cuddles then turn to double trouble
I'll make you feel good times eight
Since I'm a Terrible Influence...
I'll be the guy that you will love, feel & hate
Even be the first guy to take you on a real date

Part Three:

With or without my shirt, I still give it my best
With or without my shirt, you will lay on my chest
Listen to my heart beat fast just for you
Lying in bed as we start some banter
Escaping this world filled with trouble
Laughing and touching as we slow the chatter
Entering you slowly as we cuddle
All of your spots that will make you hot
Creating water that's bigger than a puddle
Taking over us like a tsunami
Did you think that my words would be subtle?
As you whisper in my ear that you want me

Part Four:

Do you want to know the exact moment I started to fall for you?
One day, I was in Notting Hill walking around for nothing
Thinking about you, but debating on your position on feelings
Remembering that in the end, heart plus mind will equal you
I decided to surprise you with gifts from a day of shopping
Texting you out of the blue what was your favorite red wine was
You told me and I immediately texted two of my friends for advice
To go further buying flowers and chocolate to be extra nice
Later that night, with two bottles in, we talked for a while
I'm feeding you raspberries because it made you smile
Laying with you and expressing our feelings felt easier
After round after round, you're starting to get cheekier
After we finished, lustful eyes will say she's prettier

Part Five:

You stun in shoes, pineapples, clothes, purses, jewelry (all goodies)

All the things that you deserve if you can steal my favorite hoodie

With your smiles and wiles, I can see that you aren't a rookie

You wrap me up tighter than a Teddy Bear

Swaying into sleep land from this lavender

And yet, I still say I got to have her

Quoting Musiq, we ain't to far away from our goals

Babe, you ain't too far out from my soul

Those other players will only give you that arid life

While I can promise you that Harrods life

Spending it all up as if my time is infinite

Giving me the sex that is mind blowing mental

You deserve that brand-new bag call Bental

Take you on a trip where you can ride the elephants

Only you will find these last two lines relevant

All white, you will stun them all in this chapel (yep)

All right, let's stop and drink these pineapple (cup)

#67 (The) Silver Keys (Poetic Interlude)

The Declaration of Introduction:
How do you know if you found that one?
When she promised that she wouldn't run?
How do you know if you found that one?
When she shines as bright as the morning sun?
How do you know if you found the one...?
When she stood by your side when you were at the worst?
Kissed you softly and told you that she still put you first?
When the scales finally tipped to your side from your progress?
All from being patience and then reaping the reward of success?
All of my hard work publicized and then giving her an address?
Right from the start, I will promise you security...
Holding out my hand and flashing you the silver keys...
All I ask is for you is to trust and love me faithfully...
(She's) Ready, (I'm) Set, (Let's) Go

Part One, Two, Three:
I'm known for the dark arts
Call this move Seduction
I'm known to spark hearts
Follow these instructions
All I need is a little time
To turn your night into a day
All I need is a little time
To make that little heart sway
I'm known to be on Serenade mode
Playing games, I'm going arcade mode
Because this love game shouldn't be this hard

Is your heart and mind always have to be on guard?
I feel like waging a war towards them immediately
For all your Quirks and Perks, I agree eagerly
Recklessly speaking, I'm enjoying this scenery
You and I sailing somewhere on the seven seas
Side by side, this is us as true company
When you can rock those sneakers and heels
Speaking like a preacher with nerves of steel
You and me drinking dark or from the bubbly
We can go fancy when I take you to Tuscany
On one knee, I will give you my Silver Key
Rest in my heart and read me like a diary
Of how I truly feel about you and you only

#68 (On Some) L.D.R.B.S (Long Distance Relationship Blues Story)

Part One:

I rather cheat on you mentally

Then go with her physically

Damn, that thought was scary

Damn, my mind is on empty

Mental check out, but my heart beats for you

(Re)sipping on five cups of Remy

You got me (re)playing on Demi

Leaving me fucking Lonely

No more texting, no more calling

No more sexting, no more falling

My feelings for you are at a war

Love is so cold in the winter

Losing this battle as a solider

Your love for me will simmer

I love you enough to do the distance

This L.D.R is the worst

Since your mind wrote me from existence

Everything is beyond hurt

But I still want you first

Part Two:

I will never cheat on you physically

My heart only beats for you emotionally

But you say how if I don't see you?

No one said this L.D.R.

Would be as easy as earning a star

It's the type that is made to fail?
Shouts out to those that prevails
And I swear to God it is not you
For you are what every man should want
But distance is killing me and you
Now thinking about you is a taunt
Don't say that you have made all the effort
When if I try to see you with effort?
Where is my support on that effort?
Staying in this longer than my last round
But to this, I have to cast down
I love you enough to do the distance
This L.D.R is the worst
Since your mind wrote me from existence
Everything is beyond hurt
But I still want you first

Part Three:
Maybe we should release the pain
And break us off romantically
I can't take any more of us in this strain
Can we please try and stay friendly?
'til we see each other consistently?
Dear God, don't let her write herself out of my life
Show her that we can still be together for this life
I love you enough to do the distance
This L.D.R is the worst
Since your mind wrote me from existence
Everything is beyond hurt
But I still want you first

#69 Seductress Part One: Sexy Surrender

Part One:

Hair done, nails done,

Getting me so crazy

Hair done; nails done

Wear nothing but lacy

See what I see when you stand next to me

I hear you loud and clear

From the way you look naked

I hear you wanting me near

The body is heating up, can't fake it

From the talk that has some smoothness

You got me messing up my coolness

Something like Smokey whisky

Seducing me so nicely and tipsy

Can we start this story, right?

Go and keep your pumps

Can we get to sexing all night?

Calling me over those chumps

We can even start off with a kiss

Staring you as my Seductress

Chorus:

You know that I want you so bad

Your outfits being so seductive

Even when you get a little mad

Mischief fun so destructive

Right down to your body to nakedness

You know what you are doing tonight

Just you as my seductress
Sexy time with you all alright
I need you and you need me
I'm willing to sign this treaty
This is my sexy surrender

Part Two:
The way you make me feel
This should be a naughty crime
But I'm going to keep it real
This is us justifying sexy time
Looking at you and just admire
All your lingerie so reflective
Let this erotic moment grow higher
Your sex appeal is so attractive
The way you dress so slutty
Strip like you're my favorite dancer
Treating you better than a buddy
I can really be such a romancer
Slap me one, give you the head start
Mark my body down like a chart
I just want to know how wet you are
Tell me that you want to go that far
Getting me harder and harder
Slide so well from the behind
You're ready to take on this ride
Until you get me to fall in line

Chorus:
You know that I want you so bad
Your outfits being so seductive
Even when you get a little mad

Mischief fun so destructive
Right down to your body to nakedness
You know what you are doing tonight
Just you as my seductress
Sexy time with you all alright
I need you and you need me
I'm willing to sign this treaty
This is my sexy surrender

Part Three:
Babe, don't feel so restricted
Do whatever you want to me
All that you do is permitted
When you are next to me
Wrapped around you physically
All in your head like a fantasy
Babe girl, you got what I need
That red bra, black G-string so sharp
You in the sheet is what I need
Play this next part with the harps
Just lay your head down
Start it off slowly now
We don't have any patience
We can play around and be close
Body to body with your fragrance
Let me kiss you down on your rose
Run my hands down your thighs
Sex so good, it got me in a rhyme
Get your legs up in the sky
Sex so good, it got me in a rhyme
Get your legs up in the sky
Run that line back one more time

Chorus:

You know that I want you so bad
Your outfits being so seductive
Even when you get a little mad
Mischief fun so destructive
Right down to your body to nakedness
You know what you are doing tonight
Just you as my seductress
Sexy time with you all alright
I need you and you need me
I'm willing to sign this treaty
This is my sexy surrender

#70 Quirks and Perks

Part One:
There will be times where I love you
Even when these girls got me running
There will be times when I shove you
But that might just be me bugging
Even when I know you are my lady
You might drive me a little crazy
Sometimes scratch my head and say maybe?
To that, I should bump that shit down
Against the silly things that will be annoying
You are the only one that gives me everything

Chorus:
You still give me that smirk
Even with some of your quirks
You still give me that smirk
Even with some of your quirks
Being with you has its perks

Part Two:
I know that I'm not perfect in words
Phrases and actions are the same
I know that I'm not perfect in words
Something of the run-of-the-mill game
When it's only her and me
When it starts to get predictable

Can you even believe?
We may say something indictable
But we still will remain enjoyable

Chorus:
You still give me that smirk
Even with some of your quirks
You still give me that smirk
Even with some of your quirks
But being with you has its perks

Part Three:
You know how to reverse the curse
That's why I brought you that purse
I put myself last and make you first
Love you down until your heart burst
You still love me with much interest
That's why I call you the best!
You got your ways that are unique
Against those girls, you are significant
You still give me the time and day
I'll provide you some wine and play
Whenever you act the way you are
Sexy, lovely, crazy, lady
You still are my number one star!

Chorus:
You still give me that smirk
Even with some of your quirks
You still give me that smirk
Even with some of your quirks
But being with you has its perks

#71 Caribbean Skin (Part Two)

Part Three:
Why do you have me in my thoughts tonight?
Why do you have me so high love?
I'm lingering on us getting caught tonight
Why do you look so fly love?
We were supposed to play it cool
Cause all we did was Smash,
From our many sexy travels
Your place or mine only to crash
Rule it down on your sexy gavel
Guess we were being just being Reckless
When you stay for some breakfast
Play in the sheets in your lingerie
Shining as bright as a ruby
Then only wanting me to stay
Are we simply breaking the rules?
Living in the moment where seduction and affection
Still reign to be true
It's really worth breaking the rules.

Part Two:
You're swimming so mysteriously
You're strutting around so elegantly
I'm gripping on this high on hope
All of your colors rotate into the sky
Swirling around like a kaleidoscope
And I don't even ask you why
Since we do what we do in secret
No one knows as we do it on the run

Burning up hotter than the sun
Turning everything to a scorcher

Part One:
Just like the first night that we met
But you went and made this fun
This story I will never forget
I came, I saw, and made you the one
You lead it up with a slow dance
Strip it off from this slow dance
Hands flowing down your curves
Have your body glowing so fine
Tease me up until closing time
Have your body glowing so fine
Slow it down since we are not in a hurry
Sex me down as you run this testimony
Then leave me with a kiss and your underwear
So that I can remember you in our affair

#72 No Limit (Part One)

The Declaration of Introduction:
You are trapped in your feelings
I'm such a sap when in mine...
Can we go to that place that's timeless?
Can we go to that place that let us go mindless?
Can we go to that place where my words spoken and written
is harmonized?
Can we go to that place where being carefree and we live life with
no compromise?
Some may call this better than paradise
But it's something much more to fantasize
A place that brings out the ugly, the bad, the good
Everything spoken is true and understood
Take my hand as I take you there
(She's) Ready, (I'm) Set, (Let's) Go!

Part One:
I don't even want to think tonight
So, you said let's go have a drink tonight
Take the edge off this moment
Go deep within this bottle of memories
Till the whisky and reality create the fusion
You ain't shy, unleash the color in this illusion
So, enough talk as we get in it
Tonight, we will have no limit

Part Two:

I'm fantastic in drowning in models
In this life filled with loopholes
Same notion in drowning in bottles
But trust me, I'm in total control
As you look up and say be prepared
To see our inner spirits released
To us arguing that created incredible fireworks
Round two of our inner spirits released
To us loving that created edible fireworks
Tasting your sparks deep in the dark
Resurface back in the company of stars
If they could talk, wonder what they would be saying?
(Their lives have so much regulation)
If they could talk, wonder what they would be saying?
(She's calling out on some speculation)
If they could talk, wonder what they would be saying?
(Time to set off a new revolution)

Part Three:

I'm playing on your favorite guitar
Let the Midnight Smoke Linger on
You're burning my favorite cigar
Let the Midnight Smoke Linger on
When the world gets too loud
Thoughts streaming down like a river
We can float in the ocean of liquor
Go another round of us being tipsy
The potent scent of everything savory
I know that you want to go down to win it
Even when I just want to drown for a minute
So, stretch your hands across and take a pause
Can't you hear them giving you a round of applause?

#73 No Limit (Part Two): Clock Strike Zero

Part One:

I don't want to think tonight
I just want to drink tonight
Does that make me an alcoholic?
I don't want to blink tonight
I still want to drink tonight
My mind is going catastrophic
I'm Free Falling so fast and so slow
Babe, don't leave me on this flow
Tonight, be my sexy dancer
Ignite this heart of a Cancer
I put this all on my namesake
You shake better than an earthquake
You taste better than some pancakes
Sexing sensually until the day breaks

Part Two:

Will you fly over and be my hero?
When my world starts to crumble?
Will you fly over and be my hero?
Be the one that bails me out of trouble?
Cause on some real shit,
My mind is out of sync
My mind is so heavy, it's a damn institution
On some real shit,
My pen is out of ink
This time is so deadly, I'll start a grand revolution
On some real shit,

This is how I think
It's the best type of planned solution
I'm on some freefalling mindset
I don't want to even stop time yet
In this city of Singer and Cons
The Midnight Smoke lingers on
They go on standby when the clock strikes now
The Skyscrapers shines like a prism
The colorful wavelength on the beat of this rhythm
Hope you understand now when the clock strikes zero

Part Three:
I can go on like this forever
There is no other kind of thrill
I can go on like this forever
When you and I can partake on this skill
While we try and just survive
Ready to go and pull on this trigger
Russian Roulette kind of drive
I'm just sipping and shooting on some liquor
Taking six rounds and

coming

out

of

this

story

alive.

#74 Vacancy

The Declaration of Introduction:
I wrote this story for you in dedication
Just dance for me in persuasion
Just be that girl that won't lie to me
Make this night a special occasion
Just be that girl that won't lie to me
Take away the pain that's aching me
Will you be the one to fill this vacancy?
(She's) Ready, (I'm) Set, (Let's) Go

Part One:
I can tell when I'm not feeling okay
(Thinking I got a love jones on you)
I can tell when I'm slipping away
(Thinking I got a love jones on you)
I can tell when a woman is making me sway
To tell you the truth,
I'm liking you better than myself in reality
To tell you the truth,
Is it good or bad? Well, it's about fifty-fifty
Middle fingers up to society
There goes me being a model for propriety
If that approves of you liking me
I'll renounce my level of sobriety

Chorus:

Before I taste those lips of whisky

Can you come fill this vacancy?

Before the drugs kick in the ecstasy

Can you come fill this vacancy?

Before I accidentally call you my lady

Can you come fill this vacancy?

Part Two:

All I want to do is turn off after calling you

Admitting our faults and imperfections

Come over as I burn off after loving you

Cool down and unlock a connection

I don't have any more room for this foolish world

You are worth more than rubies and pearls

I don't have any more room for any bullshit girls

I'm not trying to gas you up with shitty compliments

Just sex me up as a pick me up supplements

It's for the mutual exchange of company

To express how you and I truly feel lustfully

To you and I burn on some chemistry

Sex me down before we take a knee

Chorus:

Before I taste those lips of whisky

Can you come fill this vacancy?

Before the drugs kick in the ecstasy

Can you come fill this vacancy?

Before I accidentally call you my lady

Can you come fill this vacancy?

Part Three:

When I'm down to my last sanity
Will you appear to me a fantasy?
When I'm down to my last sanity
Will you keep me down like gravity?
Matter of fact, bring me to reality
Your sex appeal is worth the profanity
From the way you strip it down
I'll make it rain like confetti
From the way you kiss it down
Just do what you do slowly
Let your body be my serenity
Don't leave me so quickly

Chorus:

Before I taste those lips of whisky
Can you come fill this vacancy?
Before the drugs kick in the ecstasy
Can you come fill this vacancy?
Before I accidentally call you my lady
Can you come fill this vacancy?

#75 The Culture of Strippers (Poetic Interlude)

Part One:

Take center stage of this view
I see no other girl here but you
For the desire of creativity
By stripping off your lingerie
Take me higher in uncertainty
By moving around while she play
As she stays anonymously
Play your role in disguise
I won't even ask why
As her song cues her in
While she struts and spins
The roar of the men is her win
The sparks of men got your attention
Give a round of applause for your profession
Take center stage of this view
I see no other girl here but you

Chorus:

The world is her stage
When the men are engaged
The world is her stage
When the men are engaged
Against those other vultures
She does it well for the culture
When the men are engaged
The world is her stage

Part Two:

Babe, don't consider this style in shame

You know how to play this game

That's why I wrote about you in fame

Out of these girls, you are my favorite

If you're working tonight, I'm gonna make it

Pass those guys who will only decline

Give me your time and you can recline

I'll order a private room for us

Including your favorite kind of wine

Dance for me and I'll call you perfect

Those hips, your lips, I'll triple your tips

So long as you show me how you strip

Chorus:

The world is her stage

When the men are engaged

The world is her stage

When the men are engaged

Against those other vultures

She does it for the culture

When the men are engaged

The world is her stage

Part Three:

All the lights and mirrors as you're soaring in height

I'll take my seat and assume my role

You are the girl that has my eyes roaring in delight

Go on that stage and assume the pole

Bringing your style in shock and awe

Dancing for me in near beauty of raw

Girl do what you do, I won't judge
This is what you are famous for
Even when we chill after the club
This is what you are famous for

Chorus:
The world is her stage
When the men are engaged
The world is her stage
When the men are engaged
Against those other vultures
She does it for the culture
When the men are engaged
The world is her stage

#76 Whisky and Time

Part One:
From time to time I drink whisky
Then eat a piece of military gum
From time to time I drink whisky
Wait, I just said give me the rum
I got a story that has some imagery
Swimming in a sea of a thousand bottles
The breath and essence of whisky
Dreaming in a sea of a hundred models
Crashing smoothly as time ticks down slowly
Then you came and whisper to me
Just love me like you care Max
I can rock you in High Heels and in some Air Max
Just love me like you care Max
I can rock you in High Heels and in some Air Max
Just love me like you care Max

Chorus:
All I got is Whisky and Time
Care to partake on this shine?
All I got is Whisky and Time
Care to partake on this line?
Why ruin this moment in reality?
When we can play this card of mystery?
One, two, three, head to my fantasy
Just promise me your intimacy

Part Two:

From time to time I drink whisky
Then eat a piece of military gum
From time to time I drink whisky
Wait, I just said give me the rum
I got a story that has some imagery
Another dream begins in my mind
I know those stilettos when you come strolling in
You wear lingerie just to unwind
Playing the piano as a dark storm comes rolling in
The raindrops turn into rose petals
The air of the freshest flower bloom
What about the time?
(I'm running from it)
What about the wine?
(She's drinking all of it)
What about my mind? (It's Skipping…skipping…skipping)
As this record just keep (Rotating…rotating…rotating)

Chorus:

All I got is Whisky and Time
Care to partake on this shine?
All I got is Whisky and Time
Care to partake on this line?
Why ruin this moment in reality?
When we can play this card of mystery?
One, two, three, head to my fantasy
Just promise me your intimacy

Part Three:

From time to time I drink whisky
Then eat a piece of military gum
From time to time I drink whisky
Wait, I just said give me the rum
I got a story worth the imagery
My glass remains full and I'm on empty
I said don't leave me so quickly
Her red lipstick on the empty glass
She said don't worry about me babe
I'll make this a night to remember
Just show me some love maybe?
Tell the world to leave us alone
Babe, you are the Queen on the Throne
The Red Bra that has me bounded
The Black Heels that has me grounded
All the tricks you do only for me
I promise to make it rain forever
As you dance for me for my Sexy Surrender

Chorus:

All I got is Whisky and Time
Care to partake on this shine?
All I got is Whisky and Time
Care to partake on this line?
Why ruin this moment in reality?
When we can play this card of mystery?
One, two, three, head to my fantasy
Just promise me your intimacy

#77 Hold My Soul (The Alternative Version)

The Declaration of Introduction:
You think I wouldn't figure it out?
All your indecencies when you call them conspiracies
You think I wouldn't figure it out?
Looking up and down like What's happenin'
Girl, shut up. You know that I'm not laughing
Please don't act too surprised
To our relationship that you jeopardized
Suddenly, your hearts so compromised
Don't tell me to reconsider now
Don't cry me a bloody river now
It's time to stand and deliver now
(She's) Fighting, (I'm) Writing, (Let's) Go

Part One:
You stole my choice of loving others (why?)
I rather have gone away to be with her
While you went out to sexing other (guys)
You really are such a bitch turned to a cur
Trust me, if this was told in reverse
I would put up with your curses
You are the worst when I put you first
Now you want to stop the world
When another guy has you claimed
Still want me to call you my girl?
Damn, you really have no shame

Part Two:

Can't you see through the pain you're dealing me?

Or were you more interested in him feeling you?

Why didn't you tell me that you weren't happy?

Now I accuse you of cheating and being crappy

Trust me, your tears are only making you sappy

Tell me why I should even go fight mode for you

When I really was just a one-night mode for you

Tell me why I shouldn't make you that girl

That liar, that cheater, that hussy, that loser

Tell me why I shouldn't make you that girl

Trust me woman, you and I won't have a future

Part Three:

No hate in my heart and no regret

But I'm not ready to forgive you yet

Maybe I should go out on an all-out rage

Calling you every name in the book (not yet)

Maybe I should simply turn the page

Please don't even give her the hook (not yet)

Round of applause for her on this stage

For all the acts that she played in

(The sex, the gifts and the trips// the sex, the gifts and the trips)

I fell in love with her performances

(The sex, the gifts and the trips// the sex, the gifts and the trips)

You really opened my eyes

On some Pretty little Lies

Saying all the right lines to charm this heart

Something like a Heart-Taker

Life of an Actress right from the start

Now you are a Heart Breaker
I guess with me, you were never sufficed
I'm not going to ask you twice
Get your shit and bounce out my life

#78 Flirting Spirit

The (Backstory) Introduction:
Max, Max, Max
I know that you can't duck her
Max, Max, Max
I know you just want to fuck her
(Not your style, but for this story, just go with it)
But remember the words of Tucker Max
"… the devil doesn't come dressed in a red cape and pointy horns. He comes as everything you've ever wished for…"
Let me further explain…

The Declaration of Introduction:
I know you…
We have done this dance before
I know that you know me too
We had our chance before
I gave you up for the Wrong Girl
Now I want you back for this song girl
But I know that we can only do this on the sly
But to you and your body, let's do this on the fly
I want you and I know… that you want me
Temptation is like a flower that blooms in the spring
Brings out the beauty in just about everything
Yet, your scent remains a mystery to me
As you stand as a flirting spirit
(Shh) Can you hear it?
This is the first side of our tale
Let's try this scenario…
(She's) Ready, (I'm) Set, (Let's) Go

279

Part One:

When you walk to the room
You make my words turn into a stumble
When you walk to the room
You got my mind and heart in trouble
When you walk to the room
You turn mere man into a crumble
Licking your lips with such temptation
You got him up with anticipation
Your hands on my shoulders
Rubbing them as you pull me closer
One kiss and you send me into the realm of fantasies
Creating waves of chemistries
Declaring God; the winner in your creation
Making me as whole as salvation
In this world of corruption
I'm crashing my feeling like a concussion
Flowing energies against this infatuation
Believe me woman,
You're Moonlighting as Seduction

Part Two:

The first part of this story
(You know what you are doing)
The worst part of this story
(It's you that I want to be screwing)
You created this realm full of lust against me
Somewhere in my nightmare
In this hell, you are the closest thing to Heavenly
As God is my witness
Summon me back to reality
As it took was the inhale of the scent

For me to switch from decent to dishonesty
All it took was the tale of your content
To own up all my stories like commodity
In order to be with you in the case of infatuation
Before you kiss me and leave me in devastation

Part Three:
I know that having you is a sin
So, charge it against me in shame
But forgive me in the end so we will get in
I promise to make this a fun game
Love from London, let it all begin

#79 Save Yourself (True Testimony)

The Declaration of Introduction:
This started as a letter…
To see if I can make myself better
To see the demise of my poetic talents…never
Even when trying to write this Declaration of Introduction
On my life, I've never seen the true value of appreciation
What he has done, (all the same under the sun), what she has done, (all the same under the sun)
Putting others first before me is a skill
Drinking the poison to get on the thrill
Splitting my life like Dr. Jekyll and Mr. Hyde
Who the hell are you and who the hell am I?
Recklessly, I'm speaking on this with control
Even if this is slowly ruining my soul
But in this manner, that's not this story's goal
(She's) Listening, (I'm) Truth Telling, (Let's) Go

Part One:
I might be crying out for help for myself
Turning to things to fill the emptiness
I guess that is the price of being by yourself
To not run to the conclusion of loneliness
I'm feeling creative in my blind rage
Speculative concepts on this mind's stage
I'm down to the last chances of my lives
Side stepping against all the cuts and drives
I'm dodging the last dance of those knives
Guardian Angel's checklist to keeping me alive,

Two third degree cuff burns on my wrists
All these things from my addictions
Bring them all to me as my subscription
Let's start with the basic call
The Women, The Whiskey, The Music
My goal to taste them all
I wish that I had that kind of Luxury
Based on my sexy, tipsy, and reckless decisions
Good or bad? My mind's still in a deep division
Only you know how to make me special
When I'm a beast in being dysfunctional
As me told me to make this one personal

Pre-Chorus:
I'll keep this going until I'm mindless
Even when I'm surviving all of my vices
Don't mistake my kindness as a weakness

Chorus:
From one beast to another
I'm the monster in the reflection
From one feast to another
I'll devour you up in my destruction
From one beast to another
I can make it so as if I'm reckless
From one beast to another
I'll make it so to leave you breathless
From one beast to another beast
Save yourself, save yourself, save yourself
From me.

Part Two:

I might be crying out for help for myself
Turing to things to fill the emptiness
I guess that is the price of being by yourself
To not run to the conclusion of loneliness
Fuck it, I'll take in the false memories
Grasping my last sanity on a tight rope
One made me happy for a minute
(Feeling something for a smile)
One made me sappy for a minute
(Feeling nothing for a while)
One made me crazy for a minute
(Feeling everything for miles)
I love it that I can dangerously mix all three
But this is the secret between you and me
Running into the house of redemption
I'm at this crossroad of revelation
Believing that I have an ounce of perfection
Looking for any type of deception
So many truths and so many lies
Don't even ask that question why
It's so much safer to let the times fly

Pre-Chorus:

I'll keep this going until I'm mindless
Even when I'm surviving all of my vices
Don't mistake my kindness as a weakness

Chorus:

From one beast to another
I'm the monster in the reflection
From one feast to another
I'll devour you up in my destruction
From one beast to another
I can make it so as if I'm reckless
From one beast to another
I'll make it so to leave you breathless
From one beast to another
Save yourself, save yourself, save yourself
From me.

Part Three:

Every day, we all have to roll the dice
Metaphorical or literal, we all have a vice
To bring back memories once or twice
Bring our world back together
Telling ourselves that we can live forever
Possibly slipping straight down life's slope
Just burning on the heavy shit just to cope
As we get clean like a fresh bar of soap
Remember that you are a five star of hope

Pre-Chorus:

I'll keep this going until I'm mindless
Even when I'm surviving all of my vices
Don't mistake my kindness as a weakness

Chorus:

From one beast to another

I'm the monster in the reflection

From one feast to another

I'll devour you up in my destruction

From one beast to another

I can make it so as if I'm reckless

From one beast to another

I'll make it so to leave you breathless

From one beast to another

Save yourself, save yourself, save yourself

From me.

#80 Flaws and All (I Stand with You)

Part One:

I wasn't perfect when I placed my heart for sell
(On this girl, that girl, this girl, that girl)
I wasn't perfect when we were apart in this Hell
You brought me to Heaven and made me well
That's when I started to see you as a fairy tale
That you would be the one who gets the wedding bells
You made me better than the last one
When they called you that fast one.
I didn't have time to hear them list your crimes
I had to step in and blast them
Defending you as my best friend
Even when they started to stone you to bitter shame
Then asking you to be my girlfriend
Because they knew that you would don my last name

Chorus:

This is my chapter promise to you
No matter what they say about you,
Flaws and all, you're greater than a star
No matter what they say about you,
Flaws and all, you know who you are
No matter what they say about you,
They don't even have a single clue
You're so worth it, I stand with you

Part Two:

Let them, let them, let them shout about you

They don't know what you're really about!

Let them, let them, let them shout about me

All they want to do is cast their petty doubts!

Let them call you not worthy

Your presence makes them scurry

(That's why you will stand as my lady)

Those other ladies weren't ready

Of someone like you to get it all

Go shopping on my dime and have a ball

Even when they lash out at your imperfections

It's their only method to bring the disconnection

Against you and me, but it's a misdirection

No objection, you're a piece of perfection

Chorus:

This is my chapter promise to you

No matter what they say about you,

Flaws and all, you're greater than a star

No matter what they say about you,

Flaws and all, you know who you are

No matter what they say about you,

They don't even have a single clue

You're so worth it, I stand with you

Moonlight of Seduction

(Part Two)

I'm often known to speaking in codes,

Mixing the truth and some fantasies

Down this life of bumpy roads

Moments where I did and didn't blow it

At the end of all these testimonies

Hoping that you will see through it

It's time to tell you the Third part of the truth...

Welcome to The Five Suns of Amatory III:

Moonlight of Seduction (Part Two)

#81 Sanctuary

The Declaration of Introduction:
Church doesn't mix well with whisky
(She's setting the stage right now)
So, let me paint the picture quickly
(I'm turning the page right now)
As the people sat in their seats
They came to see a girl with the muse
Bringing down anyone with a short fuse
On cue, the organ begins to play her tune
She walks down the church's hallway
Dressed in white with black heels
As if it's Heaven Golden Runway
Soul Train dance vibes as they kneel
Her back's behind the choir
Every clap, they sing with fire
Every sway, they move with desire
Rocking the core of a man's soul
Her back's behind the organs
Each side of her representing wings
Each upward wave of hand ushered the tune of a fanatic
Each downward wave of hand ushered the tune of the dramatic
She's moving elegantly as the conductor
We're sexing recklessly with no structure
Dressed in all white, does that make her innocent?
Got me thinking, is she really heaven sent?
With that body defined so well,
She gets a free pass to not go to Hell

Recklessly Speaking,
(She's) Ready, (I'm) Set, (Let's) Go

Part One:
This is what I've been craving for
All your time and presence
I'm not trying to be wasteful
This is worth saving and more
All your body and essence
I'm just trying to be grateful
To your sexy walk to your sexy talk
Babe, don't even act so playful
Smoking, Drinking, and Burning against the time
This is something like Judgement Day
Good girls go to paradise, bad girls are escaping for seven nights
Roll the Vegas Dice and tell me that everything will be alright

Pre-Chorus:
As the bells begin to chime in
You're bigger than a celebrity
As the bells begin to chime in
I call you something heavenly
As the bells begins to chime in
You dance for me seductively
Telling that you want me only
Singing to me with simplicity

Chorus:

As the church plays the musical organs,
I'm raising my hand and stomping my feet
Staring at your amazing lace
Running up and down the aisles to your beat
Kissing your amazing face
Scorching the wooden floors on your heat
Singing about you on repeat, repeat, repeat
You still rock in those Heels and Jordans
As the church plays the musical organs

Part Two:

You are the girl that's worth misbehaving for
Mixing you and me on this gin and tonic
I'm not the guy that's worth saving on the floor
The way I'm speaking is a sin (how ironic)
How can you even find me at fault?
Her sultry voice brings me to a halt
Until we bust open the tequila and salt
Then our secrets are out of the vault
One kiss and you started to get clever
Maybe we can get intimate together
When the clock strikes down to one,
Promise me that you won't run
Can we start and have some fun?
When we kiss, it's a wildfire
Your sex is as rapid as gunfire
Round after round, no misfire
Trails of fiery kisses left on my body
Church doesn't mix well with whisky
So, if you are required to go tonight swiftly,
Will you love me down once more quickly?

Pre-Chorus:

As the bells begin to chime in
You're bigger than a celebrity
As the bells begin to chime in
I call you something heavenly
As the bells begins to chime in
You dance for me seductively
Telling that you want me only
Singing to me with simplicity

Chorus:

As the church plays the musical organs,
I'm raising my hand and stomping my feet
Staring at your amazing lace
Running up and down the aisles to your beat
Kissing your amazing face
Scorching the wooden floors on your heat
Singing about you on repeat, repeat, repeat,
You still rock in those Heels and Jordans
As the church plays the musical organs

#82 (I'm That) Future Queen (Interlude)

The Declaration of Intro-lude:
Yes, Yes, Yes,
I'm the one you've been looking for
Yes, Yes, Yes,
I'm the one that you're searching for
Yes, Yes, Yes,
As our enemies paid their ransom
I took it and brought our mansion
In Manhattan, listening to soul while wearing satin
Sipping wine on their dimes, gaining time
On some Penthouse vibe, we can own it times five
Let the people come in and start the chatting,
Bring the musician in as they start scatting
About me and my ascension
Now it's time for my narration
Flipping back and forth in your book
Come find me and take a good look
There I stand before you, no words
All flesh of your deepest desire
Your love is what I require
Now let's start this fire
You say I'm poetry in motion
Sensual fire burns in the ocean
Defying all the law of reality
All your Suns, I take in proudly
(My) Finest (Hour), you won me amorously
I know your poem tactics that leaves me bare

After reading all of them, they only want to stare
Naked, but comfortable in my own beautiful skin
But through it all, I know that you deeply care
Clothed in the finest garments from my closet
All brought from your elegant kind of sonnets
As I rise from these pages and present myself
As the Grape Vine will tell you to crown me as that dame
Now it is time for you to give me all the fame
As everyone will stand and they chant...

#83 I'm (Not) Okay (Disorientation)

The Declaration of Introduction:
I'm in full support of a mental health day
Then hearing news of someone's death day
(Pause and say preach)
There will be days where you are not feeling okay…
And that's okay… (to admit it)
To Hell with this
Sick of this shit
I feel like I want to quit
Fuck it all, that's it!
(Pause)
Believe me, that's why I wrote this on a park bench in Chicago after feeling all of that
No, I don't want to see a quack
Just have to express it out in the way that I know how to do
(She's) Ready, (I'm) Set, (Let's) Go

Part One:
Running, Running, Running,
In my ear, the music is blasting
Drowning my thoughts to deaf
Running, Running, Running
In my ear, what the hell are you asking?
My sanity just took a hard left
You damn right, I'm not myself

Middle fingers vibes on emotions
I don't want to hear your commotion
Just want to finally lay my guard down
Surrendering, this shit is hard now
My heard is in a different space
Panting while I pass different faces
They don't understand how I feel
I'm breathing harder than before
I'm breathing louder than before
When they don't understand how I feel (at the core)
I'm sinking until I can't take it anymore

Chorus:
I'm not okay (I'm not okay), I'm not okay (I'm not okay),
I don't want to stay (I don't want to stay) I don't want to stay (I don't want
to stay)
I don't want to stay (I don't want to stay)
I'm not okay (I'm not okay), I'm not okay (I'm not okay)

Part Two:
Painfully, it's so hard to put on a smile
After running for thirty-seven miles
Just sitting in the park to reflect on sobriety
Rather than feeling to reject everybody
Against my judgement to deflect society
(Pause)
Tasting that sweet elixir of Disorientation
As it is killing me physically and mentally
Making me curse more than about seventy (minutes)
Somehow, I'm laughing hysterically (init?)
Somehow, I'm screaming manically
I'm loving this ride of calamity

I just want to make myself very clear
"What's wrong" is not what I want to hear
Or say that "it will be alright soon" dear
Just give me a hug while I'm fighting violence in utter silence

Chorus:
I'm not okay (I'm not okay), I'm not okay (I'm not okay),
I don't want to stay (I don't want to stay) I don't want to stay (I don't want
to stay)
I don't want to stay (I don't want to stay)
I'm not okay (I'm not okay), I'm not okay (I'm not okay)

Part Three:
There will be days (where you won't be smiling)
And that's okay (just to be crying and sighing)
There will be days (where you won't be smiling)
And that's okay (just to be crying and sighing)
Cause shedding tears will bring some feeling
Even yell out loud fuck this world man (Just one of those days)
And that's okay, (And that's okay) And that's okay, (And that's okay)
If you don't agree with me, then that's okay
Just raise your fist up and let me hear you say

Chorus:
I'm not okay (I'm not okay), I'm not okay (I'm not okay),
I don't want to stay (I don't want to stay) I don't want to stay (I don't want
to stay)
I don't want to stay (I don't want to stay)
I'm not okay (I'm not okay), I'm not okay (I'm not okay)

#84 Heart's on the Run

The Declaration of Introduction:
Since when did you become a contest?
One hundred women to choose
They said I wouldn't get to you
Not on the draw, the win, just lose
Since when did you become a contest?
To see which one will have you smitten
Seriously, forget about the fallen and listen
Babe, you know how to love yourself
I want to be down with you, more or less
Tell those other niggers they can carry on
But if I must fight for you, then start this marathon
(She's) Speculating, (I'm) Competing, (Let's) Go.

Part One:
You got me spinning my wheels
From your head to the toes
You are winning in those heels
Tell me anywhere you wanna go
So many girls and so many foes
So many turns and they crashed and burn
Those other women couldn't even compete
You even got me thinking of pressing delete
I see you walking around like you own the party
Making premium deals, you're such a boss lady
Pure gossip style; they're running their mouths
Just say the word and I'm right by your side
Like Pote to Teresa in Queen of the South
Anywhere, anytime I'm down for the ride

Chorus:

At the sound of the gun,
My heart went on the run
From the night to the sun
My heart went on the run
At the sound of the gun
Babe, this is will be fun
To beat those guys in this race
Have you crown me in first place
Win it all and to kiss your face

Part Two:

So many girls came to my life
Giving their all for just one night
Until I met you and fell on that night
Flying to you to see you in that lace
Going all around the world, what a race
I know that you love this type of chase
Now, I just want to stop the whole world
Skip the travels and wine and dine you girl
You fuel my interest with your sex and fire
Even more of your smile and wiles of desire
The world, the planets, the Grand Tours
You deserve it all and much more

Chorus:

At the sound of the gun,
My heart went on the run
From the night to the sun
My heart went on the run
At the sound of the gun
Babe, this is will be fun

To beat those guys in this race
Have you crown me in first place
Win it all and to kiss your face

Part Three:
When this love chase is over,
I'll meet you at the finish line
When this love race is over,
I'll meet you at the finish line

            Sing it again!

When this love chase is over,
I'll meet you at the finish line
When this love race is over,
I'll meet you at the finish line

Chorus:
At the sound of the gun,
My heart went on the run
From the night to the sun
My heart went on the run
At the sound of the gun
Babe, this is will be fun
To beat those guys in this race
Have you crown me in first place
Win it all and to kiss your face

#85 Recklessly Speaking II: Reckless Renegade

Part One:

Sometime after writing five new stories,

Drinking about…six or seven Dark N' Stormies

She came into the bar around 20:40

She introduced herself as Aphrodite

In that tight white dress, Onyx Heels

Confidence in the style of "Try Me"

Well I'm impressed; nerves of steel

Flawless olive skin, porcelain smile

Old School Romance isn't her style

She said she would make it worth my time

Endless sex was her offer, just two conditions

Teasing me on this, let's match her proposition

One courtesy kiss, we exchanged digits

By day, we kept it cool on our visits

Then at night, did the naughty and the explicit

Two Conditions; first, only when she wants it

Second, just don't say in the end you'll miss it

Part Two:

Every time I'm at her place, she's in lace

Guess that's the price of being in her grace

She said I'm the best in the sheets

Just keep the feelings down low

I said her body and sex ignites the heat

Just keep your body cumming (go)

This wasn't supposed to last this long

But she sends me pictures when I'm gone

I'm coming over and becoming her favorite song
All she wears is her T-Shirt and Panties on
When we binge, drink, grind, and ride
All the things we do to each other… not lenient
She becomes much more than a sexual deviant
Here comes the unexplainable lapse of judgement…
(Pause)
Cursing and curving in public to hide it
Secretly sexing when we backside (shit)
Fueling on seduction and obstruction
Repeating at the seaside, its reckless
No amount of the Women, Whisky and Symphony will fulfil the deed
Her Swirling Scent of Perfume & Alcohol has become my kind of speed
She's dangerously becoming that woman I will swear that I will need

Part Three:
She's giving me instruction,
Justifying our playful aggression
We're ignoring all distractions
She's craving for my expression
Tasting her Flavour of Femininity
Going deeper in her to satisfy
Breaking her off like chopsticks
Deeply covered in her lipstick
When she leaves, it's homesick
But she laughs and said keep this fun
No titles and making me 'the one'
Girl so cold, but the sex is forgiving
Yet, Part four isn't worth grieving

Part Four:

It was all good about four weeks ago

Her feelings finally switched up in a snap

Now's she's ready to blow

Guns blazing, busting a cap

The bitter price of sexing deadly

Which side do you really want me on?

Took the back of love and let Lust drive?

She kicked them both out and locked me in the ride

She pressed the gas pedal down

Going 80 in a 30-mile zone,

Threw out both of our phones

Speeding with no desire to stop

Trying to escape from this nightmare

One night of the introduction to smash

Will lead me to destruction to crash

(Pause)

Gripped the side handle of the car,

Praying she won't kill us in this car

One set of breaks, she slammed on it

For goodness sake, ah damn it

Whip crash, but no backlash to her

But this is what I must ask her…

How could she let this go this far?

One slap, she left me with a burning scar on my face

My car totaled; she didn't even say to hold her

She smiled while burning my cigar in her lace

Against all these future bitches,

I will always be the only one who fulfilled all our wishes.

#86 A Million Rhymes

The Declaration of Introduction:
This Game of Life, I don't even have a Clue
But I got that bad case of the Déjà vu
This girl, that girl, damn I want to stay true
Yes, I'm with her, but thinking of you
Now I must break it off with her
And be called that bitch of a cur
Breaking hearts isn't my style
But without you, what's the point to smile?
This dose wasn't meant to spark up
I'm just getting so caught up
Chasing clouds while being the clouds
Skies turned grey when I didn't want to face you
You came to give me one last chance to chase you
(She's) Listening, (I'm) Running, (Let's) Go

Part One:
When you first walked past my way,
Body with the best features with fly sneakers
You became my fresh air on this day
My mind and heart automatically approved
When it came to seeking someone like you
Beauty that came from the Heavens
Brains that will always be driven
Can I roll with you on this seven?
All my old ways of love, on you I want to improve
You became a new song to sing with a touch of groove
80's vibes or 90's vibes, just keep the vinyl spinning

When it comes to you, I'm Recklessly Speaking
When it comes to you, I'm Colorfully Spraying
When it comes to you, I'm Poetically Writing
Every day I stand with you breathing
I swear I won't be leaving
To those other ladies, I won't be drafting
Right hand to God, I'm not gassing
Just keep me around, I'll keep you laughing

Chorus:
Babe, with a million rhymes,
I would drop a million dimes
To have you around a million times
Babe, with a million rhymes,
I would drop a million dimes
To have you around a million times
Babe, with a million rhymes,
I would drop a million dimes
To have you around a million times

Part Two:
Whatever you want, whatever you need
I'll give it to you in a breakneck speed
From the sky so blue
To the moon so bright
Loving you is out of sight
Babe, you are my Queen
From our friendship to our relationship
All we can and will do with a snap of a finger
Let's move on with our lives with no linger
The stars are aligned and precise
On my lucky roll of the Vegas Dice

Thanked the heavens, you're my Seven
On my lucky roll of the Vegas Dice
You've become my perfect vice
I don't even have to think twice
All in my mind all day and by night
Travel overseas as we take flight
Anywhere you want to go with delight
I want you as the earth is spinning
I need you as the sun is glowing
Give her that crown with the jewels shining
Babe, I only want you, you, you, you
Everything on my life, it's all for you
Let me be the one to make it all come true

Chorus:
Babe, with a million rhymes,
I would drop a million dimes
To have you around a million times
Babe, with a million rhymes,
I would drop a million dimes
To have you around a million times
Babe, with a million rhymes,
I would drop a million dimes
To have you around a million times

Part Three:
Real talk, you are the one that fills the void
All my past thoughts of her are destroyed
With you in my life, my heart is overjoyed
This is true as I decide to unfurl
My world won't be the same without you girl
Money don't mean a thing when we're spending

(On the time, the pictures, the gifts, the dinners)
Power Couple Status babe, we're Trending
(On the time, the pictures, the gifts, the dinners)
Even when these girls are appealing,
They are not worth me repenting,
You will always be worth protecting

Chorus:
Babe, with a million rhymes,
I would drop a million dimes
To have you around a million times
Babe, with a million rhymes,
I would drop a million dimes
To have you around a million times
Babe, with a million rhymes,
I would drop a million dimes
To have you around a million times

#87 Four Rounds Later...

The Declaration of Introduction:
Sex Dom, you are my mistress
While you whipped the air with a snap
Barked the order to get down to business
Wearing only black and red as you strap
Me down like nobody's business
You think that you are so clever?
Blindfolding me to begin this endeavor
Imaginations based on your narration
All I feel is darkness and hot pink
What is that? Well, stop and think
My blindfold is ripped off…
Watching you strip it all off
Naked Form that drives me until I'm warm
Him and I are both no longer on guard
One deep kiss before you slap me hard
Flogs, Paddles, and hot candle wax
Bring me down to my knees
Wrist burns that you can handle Max
Back scratched; skip the formalities
(She's) in Charge, (I'm) Obeying, (Let's) Watch

Round One:
I've been through the endeavor
So that we can feel the release
Something like a Sexy Surrender
One of my many showpieces
Cold steps on my chest brings the excitement

Give me your heated gaze

Touching your body slowly on this movement

Give me your heated gaze

Right after you put me in *Bondage*

Then I'll give you full homage

I love my women; Dark and Stormy

Shout out to all the ones that's down for me

Filled with energy; Dark and Foamy

I'm talking about you in that line my lady

Something we both can give and get

The simple pleasures when you're wet

Make this night something I won't forget

Babe, put some mileages on my tongue

Give it to me right as you go 101

Keep that cherry popping like gum

Tasting sweeter than premium rum

Palms pressed down to hold me right there

Playing Sex on Rotation on a loop

Just a Touch of Love babe, call me your Slave

Ride me up and down in this coop

Until you get my mind deeper than a grave

No more talk babe, time for some action

Start the walk babe, time for some passion

Round Two:

When you scowled that I need to be *Disciplined*

Just promise the reward's better than cinnamon

Come bring me your softness

Implicit desires broken tonight

Come bring me your madness

Implicit desires broken tonight
Bring me back down to my knees
On your quest to be satisfied
When I read your erotic words,
My pupils dilate
The savory combination of Perfume and Alcohol
Bound us down to the will of sex and lust on call
Keep the top and lose the bottoms
Having you shaking up to the spine
My tongue signing on the dotted line
You're such an erotic literature
Thanking the stars, it's not a dream
Tongue whips until you scream
That's my sensual signature
Kissing your stomach until I reach your lips
Sexing you until your mind goes on a trip

Round Three:
Damn those other guys that's on a budget
On Eros, you are my favorite subject
Acing your body test, tell me that I'm the best
I can make you smile more than a six-piece nugget
All the moaning and groaning,
When should our sex ever be silent?
All the cursing and swearing
Make it so loud, it's hot and violent
Recklessly Speaking, it's Sex on Poetry
Your name in the lights my dear Roxy
Razzle Dazzle me on your moxie
Yes, I promise I'm being cocky
When I'm playing *Submissive*
Time for you to become vicious

Babe, I'll give you all the fame
When I'm screaming your name
Erasing all the past girls to shame
Until I reach the core of your flame
Make you say three times you came

Round Four:
On my life, you're a blessing, you're a healer
When it comes to sex, you're my only dealer
Two wrist burns… I'll take on some *Masochism*
Even when I'm losing all kinds of feelings
Your kiss will equal a new level of caffeinism
Have you tried sex on the ceiling?
No gravity, endless intimacy
Sweet oblivion, sweet invitation
Get you started against the wall
Then have me stare and crawl
On the floor to you naked
Teasing me until I can't take it
We're so beyond crossing the line
Push me down and start your race
Downing that whole bottle of wine
While I'm doing circles from place to place
Until you have enough and need to rest
That's where you can lay on my chest

#88 The Second Piece of My Heart

The Declaration of Introduction:
You're honestly better than a snack time or a nap time
Childish tone, but that's how I feel around you babe
Real quick, do you remember your nickname?
Time to lay it all down for the last time…
I'm not a rolling stone
I'm wrapping my arms around you like a bow
I'm biting your cheekbones
Friends comes and friends go, but this I know
I'm writing this last story about you as a vow
One day looking across each other to say wow
Time for me to start your poem right now…
One shot of pineapple and I won your heart
Double Shot of Pineapples…let's call it a restart
Third time…
I heard you in your #Latenightdeclaration
Hope you still stand by those feelings
Physically, I'm on the ground kneeling
At the time of writing this final story of you…
Can you imagine if I asked you those famous six words?
(She's) Deciding, (I'm) Waiting, (Let's) Celebrate?

Part One:
Okay, you need companionship, I need companionship
Let's listen to Demi and Let's Ruin the Friendship
The late nights to the date nights watching the movie Game Night
All the times that we spent together are the ones to remember
Who knew that one day that I would get this right?

Waging war on your feelings as I broke your walls (of opening your heart)
Who knew that one day that I would get this right?
Waging war on your feelings as I took the fall (of polishing your heart)
Blame it on the tequila, (blame it on the tequila), blame it on the tequila
One more round and then we drink a margarita
I'm the writer, so follow along on this narrative
While I call you out by the styles of adjectives
Compassionate,
     Understanding,
          Remarkable,
               Intelligent and Well-rounded.
Okay, Okay, Okay,
Falling in love is scary
Can we all admit it?
Maybe, Maybe, Maybe,
Falling for you is crazy
Fine, fine I admit it
When your mom deemed us an uncoupled couple.
Physically not present, but still have feelings
Right hand to God, I still find you appealing
When we make out, my head is under water
Going deeper and deeper for your feelings
In Buffalo, NY… With you, I'm in a Good Place
Simply from first base, second base to third base
Out of my past ones, you've become my favorite
Look at me babe and tell me if I made it

Chorus:

No matter the circumstances,
You're the Second Piece of my Heart
No matter the circumstances,
You're the Second Piece of my Heart

No matter the circumstances,
You're the Second Piece of my Heart

Part Two:
Swimming through my thoughts of you
Making grill cheeses for both me and you
A smart man would wife you up immediately
Good, bad, indifferent, I still choose you
In any style to write about you notoriously
All in all, I love you when you are silly
You got me floating around like a lily
Laughing with you with no fear
As if all those girls seem to disappear
Sometimes I like you when you act so crazy
I love you when you proudly stand as my lady
Power couple style, they all look and say damn
You love me when I proudly stand as your man
Darling, you're as sweet as taffy
To you only, I'm selfish like Daffy
Cause you're mine, mine, all mine
Citing you love me for my personality
And I love you and you so incredibly
Four stories, you broke the record
Something like winning an award
As I stand for you and your hand
Read this last line like a scoreboard
A *One Woman Man* is where I stand

Chorus:
No matter the circumstances,
You're the Second Piece of my Heart
No matter the circumstances,

You're the Second Piece of my Heart
No matter the circumstances,
You're the Second Piece of my Heart

Part Three:

Those past dames, they don't get this fame
I ask you babe to finally take my last name
All white, you will stun them all in this chapel (yep)
All right, let's stop and drink these pineapples (Cup)
Only you will find these lines relevant
#Sixty-Six, #Eighty-Eight it's all evident
You get all my love and the security
Give you a future and more memories
See me as the man with confidence
Who can give you that happiness
When you feel down and out
Remember this with no doubt
You and me, we work together
Against all odds, we have the rest of our lives
You and me, we work together
Against all odds, we have the rest of our lives

Chorus:

No matter the circumstances,
You're the Second Piece of my Heart
No matter the circumstances,
You're the Second Piece of my Heart
No matter the circumstances,
You're the Second Piece of my Heart

#89 Her (Slow) Storm (Interlude)

The Declaration of Intro-Lude:
When the clouds being to form
I've never felt so alive
The smell of a majestic storm
Under the reflection of sapphire sky
The sensitivity of a majestic storm
Under the reflection of topaz sky
The music's playing inside the dorm
Under the impression of slow jazz
The crashing waves in my ears
Washing away all my fears
As the palm trees blow in quickly
The warm sand brushes my feet
Her (Rain) Dances welcome curiosity
As she enters in the next testimony
Calling me to embrace the dark wonders
Before stripping me down in the thunder
She whispers in my ear elegantly…
Welcome to my Slow Storm
(She's) Preparing, (I'm) Cheering, (Let's) Go

#90 Her (Rain) Dance

The Declaration of Introduction:
I know what I do isn't the norm
But will you join me in the storm?
I mean seriously…
Who doesn't love a good storm?
I wanna go (in the rain)
This might get a little crazy
I wanna go (in the rain)
Even before you do the Hurricane
Let's go for a ride out in the rain
(She's) Ready, (I'm) Set, (Let's) Go.

Part One:
This is your entrance…
Take a ride with me to the park
The clouds are rolling in the light
Side stepping giving me the spark
Let your moment come in right
Let the rain come pouring (down)
When you dance, you're soaring (now)
When I applaud, you're scoring (wow)
The world stops when you strut in
Center stage girl, no one can butt in
As you sway your body like a clock
Tick tock, tick tock, tick tock
As you sway your body like a clock
Tick tock, tick tock, tick tock
All dressed in black or burgundy

You know how to keep it low-key
Easing everything like a remedy
Touch your hair and your curves
Bringing shocks to my nerves
One step and you ring in the natural thunder
Bringing wonders like a sensual master
Body rocking like a natural disaster
Got me and my heart as your runner
Scratch that, enlist me as your gunner
Sex me down until we both slumber

Chorus:
Girl, you got me so blown away
In the rain, the sleet, the snow, the hail
Tell me that you are down to stay
Tell me that you won't go or bail
Don't dance for those dummies
I'll keep your days nice and sunny
You're as pure as milk and honey
Break it down…
I wanna go (in the rain)
This might get a little crazy
I wanna go (in the rain)
Even before you do the Hurricane
Let's go for a ride out in the rain

Part Two:

Take a ride with me to the park
The clouds are rolling in dark
Take a ride with me to the park
Lightening giving me that spark
Let the rain come down pouring (down)
When you dance, you're soaring (now)
When I applaud, you're scoring (wow)
Your body sways like a ringing bell
Ding, dong, ding, dong, ding, dong
Your body sways like a ringing bell
Ding, dong, ding, dong, ding, dong
Way to be in control of this song
Working hard on a nine to five shift
Shaped drum as you bring the maelstrom
Work me out as we go into mid drift
Body so cold, you bring in the snow
Body so bold, you bring in the heat
Sexy tempo when we play in the sheet
Freaky schizo when you drink it neat
When the clock strikes down,
I still put this on my namesake
You shake better than an earthquake
You taste better than some pancakes
You make me feel so much better
When I'm dancing in your weather

Chorus:

Girl, you got me so blown away

In the rain, the sleet, the snow, the hail

Tell me that you are down to stay

Tell me that you won't go or bail

Don't dance for those dummies

I'll keep your days nice and sunny

You're as pure as milk and honey

Break it down…

I wanna go (in the rain)

This might get a little crazy

I wanna go (in the rain)

Even before you do the Hurricane

Let's go for a ride out in the rain

#91 Honeycomb

Part One:
Girl, why should you and I wait?
Time moves so quickly, and everyone needs some company
We should get drunk and celebrate
The way we're staring at each other's bodies
Surfing on the waves of contemplation
Entering the realm of temptation
No titles of "yours and mine"
No complications, we can do all the things on our minds
Watch you model girl, I got the time
Give you all the finest types of wine
Anytime you want it, here's my number
We don't have to be the type of forever
We can keep it cool and just be whatever
I take the chance as you strip it down
As you dance, I promise to tip you right now

Chorus:
Drinking in your aphrodisiac wine
Sweeter than fresh honeycomb
Driving your nails down my back
Going deeper in your pleasure dome
Running your love on me on this track
We can get drunk on some wasted time
When I just want to feel your flame
Whispering your name to be tame
Promising that you are not a game
Sexing you longer than your first name

Part Two:

Girl, why should you and I wait?

As we both quickly begin to undress

I can be that man that can keep you straight

Only promise me your figure and your eight

Just keep this mind as we simply progress

On my life, you will get authenticity

For the night, unleash your Femininity

Give me the green light to your intimacy

More drinks and smoke to take off the edge

Blowing on some colorful coronas

Revealing our tasteful personas

Breathing in your body's freshness

As you turn down the sun tonight

Swimming in your yoni's wetness

As we burn up on this fun (alright)

Touching and kissing while lost in the bed

Panting and swearing with back scratched

Declaring me as "No Strings Attached"

I'm down for that babe, just like that

You get some and I get some as we feel

Just tell me if you want to be on this deal

Chorus:

Drinking in your aphrodisiac wine

Sweeter than fresh honeycomb

Driving your nails down my back

Going deeper in your pleasure dome

Running your love on me on this track

We can get drunk on some wasted time

When I just want to feel your flame
Whispering your name to be tame
Promising that you are not a game
Sexing you longer than your first name

Part Three:
After we finish the sound,
We're laying down curiously
After we hit the ground,
Miraculously, we're singing languorously
Was this Alcoholism or realism?
(Our lips taste of a slow burn)
Was this Alcoholism or realism?
(Our lips taste of a slow burn)
Something sweet and smokey
Sex you crazy or call you my lady?
This heart's going on some kind frenzy
Deep down, I know I can't have you both
When Lust got me by the throat
When your body's covered in roses
Anything you say and anything goes

Chorus:
Drinking in your aphrodisiac wine
Sweeter than fresh honeycomb
Driving your nails down my back
Going deeper in your pleasure dome
Running your love on me on this track
We can get drunk on some wasted time
When I just want to feel your flame
Whispering your name to be tame
Promising that you are not a game
Sexing you longer than your fast name

#92 I'm (Not) His... (Another Poetic Interlude)

Part One, Two, Three, Four:

I'm not his, but he wrote this about me in this sonnet

I'm not his, but he has my mind up in space like a rocket

I'm not his, but he did redo my entire closet (I'm being honest)

Triple Mirror Reflection enhances my true Amatory

For his eyes only... is the mutual agreement

From my expensive dresses, my shoes to my lingerie set

He calls me not a woman... but a beautiful achievement

I'm not his, but he keeps me in true protection

I'm not his, but he loves when I speak seduction

I'm not his, but he took me out to dinner

I'm not his, but he let me keep his Spinner

I'm not his, but I did let him come home that night

I'm not his, but I told him that we can keep this tight

I'm not his, but he smiled and kissed me with delight

I'm not his, but he cooked me breakfast with much effort

I'm not his, but he makes me laugh & drives me to work

I'm not his, but he admitted that I'm the girl in Quirks and Perks

I'm not his, but he checks on me in the morning and evening

Against the other guys, he's the only one remaining...

I'm not his, but he insisted that we go shopping

I'm not his, but he loves me in fitness mode

Having that right amount of thickness (that's his code)

I'm not his, but he keeps me well in the black

I'm not his, but he sings about me on his tracks

I'm not his, but he keeps all my bills in check

I'm not his, but he uplifts me when I feel like a wreck

Everything he does, he said to never question
Just view them all simply as love's lesson
I will never call him just a friend, but something more
I'm not his... and he will never call me Ms. Such and Such
He sweetly calls me in the evening his everlasting... Sugar Rush
All he wants is all my affection when we're together
Even if we're aren't written as forever... (damn)
Because He said I'm not his...(Woman)

#93 Grapevine

The Declaration of Introduction:
Did you hear from the Grapevine?
You are a woman that looks so fine
From your fashionable styles that shine
To my style of rhymes, you're dressed to the nine
Did you hear from the Grape Vine?
I'm looking for love in a form of a sign
Maybe Pisces, Maybe Scorpio, Maybe Cancer…
Maybe tonight, you can be my answer…
But if you can spare me a few
Let's exchange another glass of wine
I love to tell you this story that's mine
(She's) Ready, (I'm) Set, (Let's) Go

Part One:
Who are we to try and sort time?
Let's keep drinking on this port wine
We're fueled on Stardust and moon wine
I need a lifeline against this moon shine
Surfing and dodging the asteroids
Creating colorized memories (Polaroid)
Sexing until we've gone paranoid
Daydreaming about her…daily
Steady… But I'm missing Hailey
Wasn't hers; Cupid's getting lazy
Her smile is what really saved me
I write about you in high reverence
Beauty and brains are in your presence

Hope I'm not becoming a run-on sentence
But I'm more inclined to be in your essence
Your body's as smooth as velvet drapes
Hands around your waist, I want to escape
Either here or there (But's let's go to Montreal)
To a place where we swim in those waterfalls
Hear you laugh when you cannon ball
My feelings for you are in a free-for-all
Sexy Bikini flashing on your waistline
I'm slowly pushing back your hairline
One kiss and it's on your streamline
Picture perfect moment in the sun
Will you smile and say I'm the one?

Part Two:
Who are we to try and sort time?
Let's keep drinking on this port wine
Because I heard through the grape vine
You want a guy that can take his time
Not to hit you up with those petty lines
Or calling you "the one" when he's got forty dimes
You're not sure if you want me to say mine
And it's alright with me, we can just be friendly
Be cool and keep you and me so trendy
Towards this booze, let's schmooze
Laugh until our faces turn blue
Planning a trip of you and me on a cruise
Where the clouds recede to the skyline
Knock those guys who's always declining
On my life babe, you'll always be reclining

Because to tell you the truth…
I need you like a ship needs the fleet
Pirate vibes, let's just go wild
I need you like a whip needs the street
Down to ride in the night in style
Dressed in white, black, or silver in this frame
The Grapevine said to crown you as that dame

#94 Sugarcanes & Hurricanes (Main Version)

Part One:

Let's start with breaking (smitten) tradition
Recklessly, a break from (written) composition
Mentally, I might be drifting away
Daydreaming; that lingering intermission
Night surfing, mind shifting to play
All my emotion displayed on television
Babe, you are my high definition
Dark Chocolate complexion
Your thick skin for protection
That sweet juice of adoration
Taking away all my pain
Babe, you are my sugarcane
Body on point, so sharpen
Anchor on your forearm…tattoo
Curly hair tousled, eyes darken
I only want to talk about you
When you think about me only
To my heart, you can own the property
In my mind, you are the Queen on the Throne
Babe, you are the radiation of authority
Against these girls, you're mean to the bone
When everything is finally set in stone
Will you star in my next testimony?

Chorus:

Sugarcane and Hurricanes is your form

Clap your hands and let's start a storm

Drinking that sweet sugarcane,

I'm ready to truly entertain

Tonight, let's really go insane

Ride that locomotive gravy train

Let's run straight into the hurricane

Releasing all this mortal pain

Letting it go as we fall, fall, fall

Part Two:

I'm chasing for your sensation under this kinetic dominion

Can you really fault me for this kind of poetic obsession?

Your presence is as strong as Cuban coffee beans

Watching you model in on the silver screen

Spinning my head like a Vegas slot machine

You're filling my energy up like tangerine

Burning this moment faster than gasoline

Before we exchange matching golden chains

Let the sex between us become a hurricane

When you put it down babe

You're as bad as Mazikeen

Claw my back like a wolverine

Swimming deeply as we breathe in slowly

Listening deeply to Jill singing Crown Royal

Rephrase…Sipping neatly on Crown Royal

While my hands glide around your waist

Scorched alive when I go deep with no haste

Both lips, give me just one more taste

Chorus:

Sugarcane and Hurricanes is your form
Clap your hands and let's start a storm
Drinking that sweet sugarcane,
I'm ready to truly entertain
Tonight, let's really go insane
Ride that locomotive gravy train
Let's run straight into the hurricane
Releasing all this mortal pain
Letting it go as we fall, fall, fall

Part Three:

I understand that nothing last forever
So, if this is our last night together
Please leave me with a fiery kiss
So, my heart won't entirely miss
You when you go back in the storm
Partying beyond the point of reality
(I'm loving this sense of fortune)
Burning beyond the point of empty
(I'm loving this sense of fortune)
Going on the last sense of sanity
(I'm loving this sense of fortune)
That's how you'll be living lyrically

Chorus:

Sugarcane and Hurricanes is your form
Clap your hands and let's start a storm
Drinking that sweet sugarcane,
I'm ready to truly entertain
Tonight, let's really go insane
Ride that locomotive gravy train
Let's run straight into the hurricane
Releasing all this mortal pain
Letting it go as we fall, fall, fall

#95 Something Different

Part One:
I'm looking for something different…
Burned out on this fire and desire
From these past girls all liars
On the snake shit turning stones
Thinking that they deserve a throne
From my love, let's call it a loan (for the hell of it)
Now I just want to be left alone (for just a minute)
I just want someone that will give me that real
Not someone that I want to cut a deal
On something that is tangible to see it reveal
Girl, I want to see you out of this crowd
But my head is all the way in the cloud
Girl, I don't want to lose you in this round
Will you level me straight to the ground?

Part Two:
Girl, I'm looking for something different…
Not me praising you, but you do it for me
Not like a God, but when life gets hard
Words of Infatuation, Words of Seduction
Words of Dalliances, Words of Devotion
Rarely speaking on Words of Separation
These are my Five Suns of Amatory
Feed them to me for my enrichment.
I'm looking for something different
Where you check on me on the daily
Even if I don't call you my lady

Hold me accountable on my grind
So, you will have me for any time
What I really want from you is
See Me as I See You (remember this line.)
Girl, I want to see you out of this crowd
But my head is all the way in the cloud
Girl, I don't want to lose you in this round
Will you level me straight to the ground?

#96 A T.O.A.S.T to You...
(Token of Appreciation Sunflower Testimony)

"Wow you'd be willing to do a shopping spree for 125 seconds?
Maybe you are the better choice."

The Declaration of Introduction:

Plucking petals, it's part of this plot
(She loves me, she loves me not)
Plucking petals, it's part of this plot
(She loves me, she loves me not)
Just some food for thought....
In this Declaration of Introduction,
You deserve this recognition.
Let's call you... Helianthus
This one is written in my style
Just to see you...smile
Fantasy flirting with you in my head for one hour
Then, in reality, I'm (finally) buying you sunflowers
All just to see that famous look
That one that really got me shook
To be honest with you in this part
Hoping one day, I land on your heart
You embrace me softly as I start
(She's) Ready, (I'm) Set, (Let's) Go

Part One:

Something of a vibrant flower
This is where you start to grow
Calming vibes of a rain shower
This is where you start to show

347

It's Showtime girl, Rise to the Affair
Up from this concrete playground
That long, delicate stem of a body
You are this poem… hands down
Bold, elegant, and poetic imagery
Waves of being a cape of good hope
With colored patterns in symmetry
Aren't you such a kaleidoscope?
Beautiful either straighten or curly
When the sun shines on your petals
A breath of fresh air on a Monday
Eros says she's something special
Listening to My Weed Chic by Sunny Bo
Chilling at the Kensington Park
The way we can make that money flow
Chilling at the Kensington Park
Conversations that's holistic
Just us on our one on one talks
You Crazy, Sexy, Cool Brainiac
Always keeping it 100; fantastic

Part Two:
Penny, Penny, Penny, Penny
It must be my lucky day (Hey)
Penny, Penny, Penny, Penny
Let's go outside and play (Yay)
Hanging out with you until zero hour
As we go three or more rounds
I'm way better on that whisky sour
As we dance around and around
You're my favorite type of happy hour!
The way you make me feel so fly

You got that L.A Magic by Fingazz
At this point, I don't even ask why
You got that vibe like Smooth Jazz
Igniting and lingering that Midnight Smoke Legacy
That's why I wrote about you right here in harmony

Part Three:
Now for the Token of Appreciation…
Recklessly, Poetically, Sexually and Honestly
Half and Half to the above, but all innocently
Recklessly Speaking, I love you significantly
You are the girl I wish I knew back then
I can take on being one of your dear friends
Girl issues, you offered some advice for me
Some that were for gassing, others that was baffling
Man, that was fun as I look back simply laughing
For that, I say thanks for being so nice to me
You are the flower in my life worth keeping
Hope this fourth part gets your heart leaping

Part Four:
On (pretty much) everything…
Straighten hair that makes you fun
Why would I even need to lie to you?
Curly hair that radiates with the sun
You give me Butterflies times two
I love your spirit and your energy
Can you hear it? With you, I'm happy
All those guys can only give you their speeches and dreams
Musically, we can chill on some Peaches and Cream
In room 112 before we switch it to the tune of Snoop
Sipping on Gin and Juice. (Yeah, I'm running a theme)

With you receiving personalized golden hoops

As I close on this muse

A Penny for your memory

Hope we make more in the future

I love you... my

Sunflower

Muse.

#97 Dark (Vinyl) Love

The Declaration of Introduction:
Our words fade on the sound of our heartbeat
To the first night where our heart meet
Our words fade on the sound of our laughter
Babe, will you star in my next chapter?
The slow rhythmical thrust sets the pace
Girl, I don't want to waste your time
But dark chocolate cherry wine is my poison
Girl, I don't want to waste your time
But dark chocolate cherry wine is my poison
Salaciously partake with me on this wine
One glass in and let's see your beauty
Two glasses in and let's call you cutie
Three glasses and let's feel you slowly
Slip of the tongue, please excuse me
I'm the guy that has that humility
Okay, I'll tone it down on the poetry
(She's) Ready, (I'm) Set, (Let's) Go

Part One:
I'm writing back to my Roots
To mentally Break You Off
I'm serving you five type of fruits
To physically break you off
Apples, Bananas, Cherries, Strawberries, Mangos
Let's set this world on fire as we do the Tango
The view of you and me in the streaks of fire
Burning all feelings to the ground

A scorching smirk across my face
When you're wearing that red lace
Cutting edge of sexual seduction
On this moonlight inclination
Concluding with pure revelation
I'm so tasteful and a psycho of infatuation
You're so playful as the virtuoso of stimulation
Elevating your pleasure as a specialty
Making it more tasteful than pornography
Let's do some shots of Sex & Photography
Frame by frame right from the start
Name by name you're a piece of art
Painting you as that woman of the Renaissance
Galleries of your pure body in the nude
Striking and reveling poses of your moods
That snarky but stimulating type of attitude
Before illuminating your euphoric pulchritude

Part Two:
Soft lips and long sighs are her vibe
Dark Chocolate Wine is what I prescribe
Dark Love on the Vinyl is what she subscribes
Stealing kisses, it's her type of bribe
Who is she? It's hard to describe
When my eyes trace every symmetrical inch of your shape
All the right curves and features sweeter than any crepe
To talk about your complexion kissed by the golden orb
But you got that on lock down
Rephrase, you're such a knockout
Your dexterity with your seduction
Will always have men in confusion

Admiring your Sexual crescendo
As a triumphant war call to only me
I shadow you with some mystery
While I have your heart smitten
So, they won't know our innuendos
Just remember them here as written

#98 Against the Wall

The Declaration of Introduction:
The way she moves from that stance
Step, step, with me on this chance
Take my hand as we begin this dance
Step, step, with me on this chance
Time to pull you into this trance
(She's) Ready, (I'm) Set, (Let's) Go!

Part One:

In this poem that started as a letter,
I will crown her something better
She will be shining for years
With diamonds on her ears
Let me make your name clear
My dear...
This fleeting time in this space
With colored pattern spots of lights
There you are within the night
In that tight white dress, glowing
A sweet melody that made you a drug
Impressed by the way you can cut a rug
Against these girls, you're my only choice
All I crave is the sound of your sexy voice
Your body on my body going sensually
Hands across your waist, we're swaying
While that slow jam song is playing
To your feelings, I'm serenading
Off the dance floor to the wall
Where we can act a little naughty
I love your perfume, so fruity
Put your hands above your head
As I give you kisses on your neck
Bringing in that soft shade of red
As I give you kisses on your neck
My hands tracing up to your thighs
I'll give you every reason to flaunt it
A sly chuckle turns into soft sighs
Just tell me slowly how you want it

#99 Satin Blindfold

The Declaration of Introduction:
I want you now sexy. Stripped down, handcuffed, and ready to be taken
Oh my gosh you have no idea how hot that is babe I want that to be one
of our realities.

Whatever my babe wants, she gets it.

I don't want you too
I need you touching me
Appreciating me deeply
Loving me down real…
Good because I need that 50 Shades style
No communication needed just cuff me
And take me knowing I want all of it.
Stripped down, handcuffed, and ready to be
Taken Down.

(She's) Excited, (I'm) Pleased, (Let's) Begin

Part One:
Babe, let's start this love affair right
Babe, take your place in this chair
Pop wine or champagne for tonight
Roll back your body and your hair
Start this mood up and be alright
One dance for you to make you smile
Are you ready for this innovative trial?
Truthfully, let's start on this dare
You accept being tied on this rope
Take this Satin Blindfold and hope
Our imagination is in the same scope
Building temptation up to the toll

Round your wrist for the pressure
Feeding you berries from the bowl
Just to have you restricted and secure

Part Two:
Massaging your head to relax you down
That warm feeling of tingling (higher)
Leaving your mind lingering (liar)
Pampering your heart nimbleness
On the sweet serenity of my sex
Shown in your hand's tautness
On the sweet serenity of my sex
Rubbing your long legs deeply
While your scent blooms sweetly
Taking your panties off slowly
Spreading your legs quickly
Breathing heavier and louder
Licking until you cum softly
I knew that I made you prouder

Part Three:
Now that I got your mind molded
Let's not keep you blindfolded
Fairy lights to cover your room
Red rose petals to call you special
Burning your favorite candles
Senses heighten and amplify
Yearning to make this a scandal
Senses heighten, let's testify
She's ready to take down her feast
When I saw her true red eye beast
She laughs, "don't you even dare"

As she broke free from her chair
She pinned me down to start her rampage
Until both of our minds started to disengage

#100 Grandiose

Part One:

After we gone seven minutes from second base
When I stare into your face, I'm lost in space
The stars in your eyes, shining infinity
Levelling my mind to normal sanity
One in a Million vibe you are babe
So angelic, so poetic, so magnetic
Bringing in the drums as you strum
These harps to smooth everything
Down to the beat for me to stay around
Cruising in limousines, bring in the tambourines
Eating jellybeans and tangerines all night long
Life is so much sweeter with you in this song

Chorus:

I would run up a hundred grand
To become your favorite company
I would run up a hundred bands
To become your favorite symphony
Play every sound to see you smile
Call you the truth, my epiphany
My number one hit, indefinitely
As I play out this perfect key

Part Two:

Musically Speaking,
When I hear your voice daily,
Not just in my many song lines

It drowns out all the crazies
I want you for a very long time
Because I know you're my lady
Fancy times when we have tea and crumpets
Fancy vibes when you and I play the trumpets
Against our hips, we can simply bump it
To my feet, you got them marching
Until the skies bring the moon
To my heart, you got it beating
Until the skies turn maroon
To my voice, you got me singing
Until the skies turn true blue
Look what you made me do

Chorus:
I would run up a hundred grand
To become your favorite company
I would run up a hundred bands
To become your favorite symphony
Play every sound to see you smile
Call you the truth, my epiphany
My number one hit, indefinitely
As I play out this perfect key

Part Three:
You're singing to me on this tune
Creating a man so differently
Then you kiss me softly and suddenly
Crowning you as my endless possibility
From London, Paris, and Rome
I'll have you engraved in history
Until I'm told to come back home

Living in peace in your symphony
Forever loving your sweet melody

Chorus:
I would run up a hundred grand
To become your favorite company
I would run up a hundred bands
To become your favorite symphony
Play every sound to see you smile
Call you the truth, my epiphany
My number one hit, indefinitely
As I play out this perfect key

THE FOURTH DECLARATION OF DEDICATION:
Memories of Dalliances and Devotion

I'm often known for speaking in codes,

Mixing the truth and some fantasies

Down this life filled with bumpy roads

Moments where I did and didn't blow it

At the end of all these testimonies

Hoping that you will see right through it…

By the end of these sessions, you will understand it all.

When you read this and see which one of us will fall.

Who are you going to believe at the end of this story?

It's time to tell you the Fourth part of the Truth…

Welcome to The Five Suns of Amatory IV:

Memories of *Dalliances* and Devotion

#101 Start Over

The Declaration of Introduction:
Have you met that man that can play the piano?
Have you met that woman that can shoot with ammo?
Have you met that woman that can rock those stilettos?
How could I forget about you in those stilettos?
When you first looked at this fellow…
You smiled and said hello to me
This must be a dream come true
Beauty and brain are her style
Let's be friends is what she smiled
I agree to just be in her atmosphere
So, I won't be that guy of yesteryear
We exchanged numbers and summers
Then seeing each other every season
Some might cite this moment a reason
That's when I knew it was over…
100 stories later… time to Start Over
(She's Almost) Heard them all, (I'm) Still Surprising Her, (Let's)
Start Over.

Part One:
Babe, hope that you would please excuse me
From the way that you got me made
From the brains right down to your beauty
To get next to you, I'll try and persuade

I'm feeling things... not that kind of lust
But rather on a "you get me" kind of trust
I can give you all of me if you let me
Show you a life that's so much brighter
Trust me babe, I'm such a writer
As I stop and go out on this whim
When I write about love, you are the synonym
To your heart, hope that you say let him in
I don't mean to rush on that line
But I only have two more parts
Just to see if I can make the mark to your heart
Or fall in the dark and simply return to start

Part Two:
Whenever you are feeling so fancy
You can buy the whole mall on me
I can roll on this notion so easy
We can do the simple things on me
To a matinee or even a symphony
Money really don't mean a thing to me
I just need you and you need me
I'll love you if you say you do to me
But we don't have to rush this now
We can just spend some quality time

Part Three:
Babe, please don't be so frantic
I'm an old school romantic
I can make you and I a first date scenario
Pulling up to your home with your favorite song on the stereo
To elegant dinners with five star desserts
To your favorite artist at a front row concert

Things to make you shine when you wear some Tiffany
By the end of this, that's how you will remember me
Riding through the city with all kinds of leisure
Don't be surprised by the end I call you my treasure

#102 Back to the Basic (Old School Romance)

The Declaration of Introduction:
When was the last time you got swept off your feet?
All those compliments that made your heart beat?
No smoke screens or prism dreams in the mirror...
Let me make myself clearer
I may not be that man in those videos
All the cars, the houses, and all those (whoa)
Make you bend over and touch your toes
That's not how this story will even go
So, ladies, listen up while I start over
I want to take you back to a time
Where money and status didn't mean a thing (almost)
Where a walk in a park or a museum meant about everything
Just a talk, to a date, to even share a kiss
Something to even reminisce
Promise you that I will not front
When I make you once more famous
We can do whatever we want
Let me take you...Basic to the Basic
(She's) Wondering, (I'm) Inspiring, (Let's) Go Exploring!

Part One:
Hey, how you doing girl?
I don't mean to interrupt your world
Just had to stop and get your name
I hope another man doesn't have you claimed
Cause I'm that man that on some good taste
Not running in the streets on some hood fate

Looking at you like babe, you the shhh…

But to me babe, you are such a gift

To your heart, I'm trying to uplift

Not rehearse a line on a script

You and I are quite the vision

In my chorus songs or in this letter

Hope you agree on that decision

I just want to get to know you better

Maybe we can exchange the digits

Promise girl, it won't be a gimmick

Might even arrange for some visits

Travel anywhere you want, no limit

Part Two:

Damn, I'm surprised that you called

Cause the way you left, it felt like you wanted nothing at all

But anyway, what are your plans tonight?

We can go to parties dressed in all white

Stand through the crowds and we look all right

I can call you up later and rent a car

One look at you babe, you're a star

Notoriously speaking, you're a fly chick

Rocking sidekick, rocking fly kicks

Or maybe we can just go on a date

To your front door with your favorite flowers

Riding until we reached the Willis Tower

Dining at that favorite restaurant

Eating and drinking till time becomes nonchalant

Then we walk arm by arm if that's what you want

Maybe even pet the doggie after the playful bark

Twice around the park, good company as we talk

On our hopes, dreams, and vulnerability

Uplifting each other to that level of invincibility,
Babe, stop wasting your time and your love
I'm not calling your bluff, but one night isn't enough
We can take this slow and be friends
To go out on one more date again

#103 I Love You... (What More Can I say?)

"A person that truly loves you will never let you go,
no matter how hard the situation is..." ~Unknown

Part One:

Why do we always argue like children?
Back and forth again and again
Seriously, why do you tell your friends?
Running to them for some advice
Honestly, they're feeding you lies
You don't want to hear what I say
Do you really want it to be that way?
Don't you know that they want us to end?
Those bitches seriously want you back with them
In the single land where they have no man!
Or worse, tell you to leave me for a new man
I promise to keep it real with you
You do the same for me times two

Chorus:

Live for today, plan for tomorrow
Girlfriend first, then maybe wife?
But time, give me some to borrow
This is the Worst Day of my Life
But we fight so much at night, we need a ref
We don't get this right, then what will we have left?
I swear by the stars that are above you... (This is the only way)
All that I know is that I Love You... (What More Can I Say?)

Part Two:

Oh no, here comes round two of this

Promise broken, all this spoken,

I don't want you around anymore

When will you and I decide to quit?

Babe, I just want you to hit the road

We can't see eye to eye, let's just split

Throw the bottles at me and scream

Dear God, let me out of this dream!

(Pause)

I guess after that we might need a breather

(Pause)

This is where we have pushed each other

But through this storm, I seek no other

You still are the one I still find passionate

Choosing you in my life wasn't an accident

Singing Robin Thicke times two

I guess the old saying is still true

Can You Believe it?

There is *Love After War*.

Chorus:

Live for today, plan for tomorrow

Girlfriend first, then maybe wife?

But time, give me some to borrow

This is the Worst Day of my Life

But we fight so much at night, we need a ref

We don't get this right, then what will we have left?

I swear by the stars that are above you… (This is the only way)

All that I know is that I Love You… (What More Can I Say?)

Part Three:

Babe, can we work it out?

I'm for you babe (no doubt)

Babe, can we work it out?

I'm for you babe (no doubt)

Name me one couple who hasn't gone through this season

It's not worth losing you

From my apartment, simply from this stupid disagreement

But it's better than our last Argument

I'm still choosing you

Chorus:

Live for today, plan for tomorrow

Girlfriend first, then maybe wife?

But time, give me some to borrow

This is the Worst Day of my Life

We fight so much at night, we need a ref

If we don't get this right, then what will we have left?

I swear by the stars that are above you… (This is the only way)

All that I know is that I Love You… (What More Can I Say?)

#104 Recklessly Speaking III: Recklessly Balance

The Declaration of Introduction:

What we are, no one can debunk

Kiss me when your lips are red

Wait, I'm starting to get drunk

Whisper to me that I'm not dead

Sipping on the finest time while wasting wine

Hope you guys didn't notice…

I just need to stay focused…

Back to the story…

(She's) Drinking and Listening, (I'm) Drinking and Narrating, (Let's) Go

Part One:

Hit me with them smokey eyes

Simply drinking up whisky lies

Truthfully, I'm really into you

A shadow of mystery for the night

Heart and mind in a gambling fight

Saner heads triumphs. Rambling right?

Let's go out and make some trouble

No hesitation, let's go on the double

Ride out with me with me while we burn the streets

You make the move while you turn on these beats

Chorus:

You're my highs and my lows

Scorching needs of endorphins

You're my highs and my lows

Rolling weed and on morphine

Chasing the light, singing this song
Dressed in desire, bring in the fire
Feelings at night, craving the wrong
Round of applause for our chemistry talents
As we keep each other so Recklessly Balanced

Part Two:
Since you became my accomplice
I'm in too deep to even withdraw
No one should try and stop this
The people only go blah blah
We're sinking in wine, but we're breathing just fine
Quick intake of inhalation on some temporary love
You and me; let's really make us legendary love
Power Couple Status, they say we're the baddest
Out on vacation, we're racking in the profits
Out on vacation, we're drinking in the tropics
Case of the love & lust; it's a win, lose or draw
(Que sera sera)
Pictures of us, let's celebrate like it's Mardi Gras
You look amazing when you're topless
Posing and dancing with sway... beautifully breathless
Posing and watching you slay... skillfully heartless
I gave this moment to you in the appreciation
When you get me on a brand-new rotation
It's time for a brand-new celebration

Chorus:
You're my highs and my lows
Scorching needs of endorphins
You're my highs and my lows
Rolling weed and on morphine

Chasing the light, singing this song
Dressed in desire, bring in the fire
Feelings at night, craving the wrong
Round of applause for our chemistry talents
As we keep each other so Recklessly Balanced

Part Three:
Before we start to crash down
On love, lust, sex, passion, let's get higher
I think we should smash now
Every moment with you, I'm getting wiser
Shoot me down with your tranquilizer
Naked body to body, perfect stabilizer
No rush to the finish on this minute
Love making style, beautiful sounds
Free falling 'till we land in the clouds
Smiling, you say that I've redeemed this round
In the end, say you love having me around

Chorus:
You're my highs and my lows
Scorching needs of endorphins
You're my highs and my lows
Rolling weed and on morphine
Chasing the light, singing this song
Dressed in desire, bring in the fire
Feelings at night, craving the wrong
Round of applause for our chemistry talents
As we keep each other so Recklessly Balanced

#105 Private Love

The Declaration of Introduction:
In the art of Introduction, there I communicate
In the art of Temptation, there she manipulates
It is venomousness of the senses
Where multi-color flames exile the moodiness
Please, please, lower your defenses...
As I come close to your lips to taste the juiciness
The pleasure, the preferences of entering...
In this spell of a thousand delights
In with you, it's a thousand nights
I run you a bath with the finest senses of raspberries
Pair with dark chocolate and wine (Tasty)
Background songs of the Grown & Sexy
This is the only thing the palace of pleasure
Welcome to our Private Love
(She's) Scheming, (I'm) Intoxicated, (Let's) Go

Part One:
Swear to me that you will not tell your friends
They won't understand what I can do for you
Swear to me that this night will not be the end
Guaranteed my love for you will ascend
All I want for you is to simply... come thru
Silence rules the circle of candles and rose petals
Holding hand across each other
Eyes deeply dilated and focused
Everything on our minds, let's do them tonight
Out of this world vibe, let's go on vacation

Let's ease our mind on this anticipation
No worries of any kind or disruption,
When I start kissing with temptation
Shall we continue this elevation?

Pre-Chorus:
Since there is no one here to disrupt this vibe, you, and me
Come around girl, put it down on me so lovely
Seeing apparitions of sensational love, your beauty
Bring your body and dance for me slowly

Chorus:
All I want is some Private Love, (Private Love), Private Love
Let's not call this a dream, Let's make it our private scene
All I want is some Private Love, (Private Love), Private Love

Part Two:
You kiss me softly and rub my face stubble,
The way that you take off your lace (trouble)
Writing you through this erotic literature
Let's continue to paint this erotic picture
You say let's do it on my furniture
Muscled arms to grab me tightly
From behind, this move is naughty
You moan and groan so deeply
Screaming in desirable ecstasy
Damn, I love this inner melody
Your scent lingers in the warm air
Babe, this is no time to hesitate
All your feelings, time to renovate
As you flip the script, my clothes are ripped

Part Three:

Pulling me close, you admire my masculinity
Burn with me on this Five Suns of Amatory
Your legs parts to show off your femininity
Massaging your inner thighs as I taste for survival
We're amorous freaks turned rivals
Thrusting in you deeply in missionary
The whole wide world goes in idle
Love making into this perfect cycle
(One more round) in this spiral (One more round)
Executed with razor sharp precision
Clawing my back to mark your signature
Claiming me in this submission
With you tonight, I made the best decision

Pre-Chorus:

Since there is no one here to disrupt this vibe, you, and me
Come around girl, put it down on me so lovely
Seeing apparitions of sensational love, your beauty
Bring your body and dance for me slowly

Chorus:

All I want is some Private Love, (Private Love), Private Love
Let's not call this a dream, Let's make it our private scene
All I want is some Private Love, (Private Love), Private Love

Part Four:

Now that I have done what you wanted
You're the best girl ever, full homage
In lingerie, you look brand new in purple
Open the night skies after sexing in circles
Moonlight glow on our skins (it's a win)

Tied to you, it feels like perfect bondage
We can get close and cuddle with ease (boo)
Hope that I did well to simply please (you)
This is what happens when you tease (boo)
This was her last decree to me
I will free your mind to oblivion
So that we can create new experience
Body, Soul and Mind, I will concentrate
Hope all my sensual words still penetrate
Babe, if you are, I am all in
As I start this round again

Pre-Chorus:

Since there is no one here to disrupt this vibe, you, and me
Come around girl, put it down on me so lovely
Seeing apparitions of sensational love, your beauty
Bring your body and dance for me slowly

Chorus:

All I want is some Private Love, (Private Love), Private Love
Let's not call this a dream, Let's make it our private scene
All I want is some Private Love, (Private Love), Private Love

#106 Sucker... (Poetic Interlude)

Part One, Two, Three:

I'm a sucker for curly hair on a fun day

I'm a sucker for straighten hair on Rainy/Days

I'm a sucker for wet hairs after a good shower time

I'm a sucker for flirty words

I'm a sucker for your curves

I'm a sucker for your intelligent mind

I'm a sucker for adventurous time

I'm a sucker for the "hair done, nail done, eye shadow" type of woman

I'm a sucker for that natural look

I'm a sucker for dark skin, light skin, basically all skins

I'm a sucker for a bright smile

I'm a sucker for all her vibe

I'm a sucker for Mini Skirts & Mini Flirts

I'm a sucker for jewelry on a woman

I'm a sucker for home cook meals

I'm a sucker for metaphorical desserts

I'm a sucker for Quality Time

I'm a sucker for affection

I'm a sucker for honesty

I'm a sucker for your Butta Love (Next!)

I'm a sucker for our banters

I'm a sucker for original jokes

I'm a sucker for that snarky but stimulating type of attitude

I'm a sucker for your level of dulcitude

I'm a sucker for being a "Hopeless Romantic"

I'm a sucker for Words of Affirmation

I'm a sucker for being a Heart Taker

I'm a sucker for handwritten letters

I'm a sucker for our make out sessions

I'm a sucker for spontaneous love

I'm a sucker for being your Love Well Spent

I'm a sucker for your expensive perfume

I'm a sucker for your unquestionable trust

I'm a sucker for your touch

I'm a sucker for your voice

I'm a sucker for your figure

I'm a sucker for your backstory

I'm a sucker for your personality

I'm a sucker for you Darling.

#107 Solace in (Erotic) Poetry (Interlude)

Part One & Two:

Vapors of memories of past and future intention

Her (Rain) Dance always leaves impressions

Drenched in written erotic words

Raising from the oasis of sex

Echoes of moans and groans

Whispering wet fantasies

Twisted perverse pleasures

The darker the romance

In this nocturnal aroused scent

The sweeter the love

In this infernal aroused scent

The darker the romance

In this journal aroused scent

Pages after pages, I write about me and you (so clever)

Sage after Sage, I burn on our love (when we're together)

Release the pure smoke of flirtation

Visions conjuring degree of imagination

Seduction, the next level of elevation

Every poem always needs a face

So, I write about you in its place

Raw Poetry, uncut and revealing

The ones that make you bite your lips

Mind fucked slowly; eyes dilated

Writing poems to breathe in desire

Let's dance on this one persuasively

The stories we will write and inhale

This is me on this level of creatively
Serenading sex like a pure desire remedy
The way I talk to you gets you to accelerate
That will be known as my surefire history

#108 (The Introduction of) Ms. Risqué

The Declaration of Introduction:
All dressed in silk with a touch of golden
No time for the fake love of broken trust
Fall on me softly like frozen dust
Blooming in twelve rounds of bouquets
Scorching well in multiple foreplays
Ride me down on this speedway
Are you ready to become Ms. Risqué?
(She's) Intrigued, (I'm) Inspired, (Let's) Investigate

Part One:
They say that you come in a style of a Dominance
Dawned in black leather bustier with a matching thong
Red bottom shoes that you brought from my songs
Standing so loud and so proud in confidence
You won't tolerate any level of ignorance
Meeting you is such a gamble
All those other guys just ramble
Tell me girl, what is your angle?
You left them all in shambles
Your style burns well like a candle
Wearing Agent Provocative, fashionably it's your style
That level of seduction, it would be rude to not stay awhile

Part Two:

Let the world go and protest our moment

As they sing Who Do We Think We Are?

Let's Live It Up like we are a couple of stars

Given their silence babe, our love has spoken

Something magical like in Second Piece of my Heart

I look at you impressively like a recess pieces type of art

The way you deal with those old fools

Throwing them back like an old school

Because that other guy is an old tool

You're that girl that keeps it so cool

#109 A House is Not A Home

Part One and Two:
Times are tough and love is starting to lose its taste
Monogamy is becoming a well-rehearsed joke
There weren't any girls that were beating for me
I was ready to start running towards the end...
Where drinking was the only answer for me
Numbness was the best feeling in the world
Since I'm not even with you girl
Without you... I'm just a stray out there
Going from here, to there, to there
Finding temporary stays for the night
Only lying to myself that it is alright
She would do it until the next day
I leave and then start this stupid race
But you only look at me and touch my face
I'm trying to run back to your grace
Pleading for redemption in this confession
Fighting depression from lack of selection
I really would renounce all my collections
But your lack in faith got me questioning
When you didn't believe me that I would return
And yes, for that it sucks and to the core burns
Where are my points (for the times) where I was waiting for you?
Where are my points (for the times) where I was fighting for you?
Ignoring those voices to let you go and walk out there?
Where nothing only brings sadness and confusion?
Ignoring my self-destruction

Justifying my single life recreation
Miniskirts and mini flirts are my type
Truthfully, it's getting pointless in my life
Feeling a bit Moody, but I'll say it as well
Just say the word and I won't see anyone else
I don't want to go anywhere except…
Your arms hold me down like an anchor
In my mind you are the only answer
After finally getting all my shit together,
On Christ, I want you as my faithful wife
Creating a new one with you and only you
Diddy and Jamie told me that we should be *Partners for life.*

#110 Vulnerability is Romance

Part One:
As my words begin to start raving
I can see it in your eyes misbehaving
On you miss Black Superfly
This is my style of this craft
Cause you're a bad mother...(shh)
I'm just talking about Shaft
I think you're such a dime
You've been on my mind
I want to hear your fantasies
Maybe make them all realities
Lights down low, play that slow tempo
She said Vulnerability is Romance
So, to her, go and take the chance
I admit it, I'm interested in a hook up
But damn it, cupid said look up
Just take her out on one date
To her clothes, too early to remove
Take it slow and keep the groove
Give her the mull wine as a spell
She kisses softly... Time will Tell

Part Two:
Before you get nasty, let's do a two-way fantasy
You imagine me anyway you want
Give your mind something to flaunt
I'm thinking... nice suit, whiskey in hand, slightly unbuttoned top...
(cheeky)

You are the opposite of simmer

If you want to hear the rest that's going to cost you a dinner

Matter of fact, be my dinner, make you cum... out the winner

Musically and Recklessly Speaking

Your kiss and your touch are brand new

Can we end the night on me and you?

Just chill on some wine to kill time

Nothing heavy unless you say you ready

Part Three:

I love when you play The Good (girl) and Bad (girl)

Either Way, with you I need *One More Hour*

On our first date, I can play the whole album

Trust me, the next line wasn't written in random

Flirting is teasing, teasing leads to anticipation, anticipation leads to the possibility of release

One kiss on the bench, it left a mark

One drip turned drenched, it's a spark

You love it when I do this kind of talk

Like Eva and Ray, can we kiss & play on the mattress?

In that moment, I don't need any practice

To kiss you further down into blackness

Fantasies of making your legs tremble

From us drinking chill wine, playing music, rolling one or two, blowing three or four, teasing is an encore

Anticipation is waiting for cookies to finish baking

But I prefer baking some brownies

While we wait, we tune in on some soul

I'll level it here until you decide to take control

#111 Cosmic Dust

Part Three:

Darkness and void were all that I saw
Hoping and praying for more chances
Until you came and ripped it with your claw
This is where you pour on the canvas
Cobalt Skies as a start before ruby elements
Festival of colors, you created my soul
Fingers gliding through the sky
Something like the Glow of Venus
Red lips with wine, curvy leanness
Meteor shower, interstellar voyage
White lightning beautifully structured
Our days together are not numbered
Sheets of stars around and colored
Celestial fires around your head
Shining dress, 600 count thread
Heavenly impress, you make me red
With you babe, I'm the opposite of dead
Coming back alive maybe once or twice
Reviving my words from this Poetic Rust
Your galaxy is the isles of paradise
Inhale with me lightly on this Cosmic Dust

Part Two:

Electricity runs through my body
When we collide together peacefully
Stellar Collusion vibes so ambivert
Mesmerized, I want to be in your galaxy

Drinking Sugarcane and Hurricane (again)
Leaving this world in this distance
We feel nothing in the resistance
When you and I reach solidarity
We can go free falling with some oxygen
Laughing and Sipping on Cosmopolitan
Reviving my words from this Poetic Rust
Inhale with me lightly on this Cosmic Dust

Part One:
When it comes to you, I levitate
The skies are so blue, let's celebrate
All of you babe I want to gravitate
You stay on my mind about 24/7
Don't listen to those men with the nonsense verse
For their time with you, don't even reimburse
I call you something beautiful like a universe
All your stars against the darkness
When you scribed your fingers in the dark
With sparkles of stardust glowing in the dark
Let's slow dance on this slow jam in the colorful abyss
Body to body, hands moving as our pulse increase
Until we start the motion of the Stellar Collusion
Free Falling into the rhythm of exploration
Reviving my words from this Poetic Rust
Inhale with me lightly on this Cosmic Dust

#112 Sketchbook

Part One, Two, Three:
Diary entries written in a Typewriter
Train of Thought on this baseline
Write it all down with the right chaser
Any drink so I do not waste time
Ride on these rhymes so you can get to my destination
But I need a new way to speak my Devotion
Pencil scripted, not of words of commotions
Scented color pencils to enhance the imagination
Do you remember your Flavors of Femininity?
Simply drawing from past vivid illustration
I sketched you in my notebook of what you are to me
Take off your dark shades and come draw me
As I welcome you in my Sanctuary
From the heat of a thousand suns
While emulating the colorful reflection
Made from your heart you say that I am a piece of art
Where I am securely framed
It gives you joy just to say it.
Something like a perfect mosaic
One mouth, two eyes, one nose, one pair of smooth legs
Outlining the curves of your shoulders
Long dark hair and two hands
Sitting on a white bench with the flowers arch above you
A lean body where a mind would linger
Bring you to real life like some relativity
Like pure lyrics are to a singer

This is what you said to me…

I heard you when you wrote about me (Get Reckless)

Time for you to stand with me (Get defenseless)

Find me in your mind as we start the connection

Bathe in my colorful warmth from the reflections

Feeling so sedated, but getting so elevated

Let's raise one up to my creation!

Let's raise one up to our celebration!

#113 See Me as I See You (Interlude)

The Declaration of Intro-lude:

Mirror on the wall…

Tell me how I should fall…

For you.

The hardest things in life are not easy,

So, going after your heart was a challenge

Shot down many times in the act of defense

I don't blame you; your mind was on duty

Your heart was told to go on the defense

So, you would have to truly excuse me

For my actions sanctioned by Eros

To run a play to become your man

Because you feel so right for me

How could you find yourself not worthy of this love?

We all need that kind of love…

I want a woman that sees me as I see her…

Rewarding

Successful,

Supporting

Powerful,

Beautiful,

Relentless

&

Resourceful

More importantly,

A woman who is

Faithful

Boldly Speaking;
I want you to
See
Me
As
I
See
You

#114 (I'm Such a...) Child At Heart

The (Inspirational) Declaration of (Conversation):

> Max likes you because of how you made me
> feel all happy on the inside.

She liked Max because of how he made her felt safe, secure, happy and comfortable inside and out no matter what...

> Max Likes You
>
> +
>
> You Like Max
>
> (Musically Taunting) Max and You sitting a tree...

The (Romantic) Declaration of (Introduction):

When it comes to you, I'm such a child at heart
(When it comes to making you laugh and giggle)
When it comes to you, I'm such a child at heart
(When it comes to making you smile from my riddles)
When it comes to you, I'm such a child at heart
(For you and I to stay for a while from your scribble)
Growing up? Honestly, I don't even want to start.
(She's) Reminiscing, (I'm) Truth Telling, (Let's) Go.

Part One:

You want to know the best part of you coming into my life?
We can enjoy each other's company without any strife
Contemplating on you becoming my wife?
Am I moving too fast? Welcome to living this life.
When you know what you want, you go and get it.
Regardless of time or people...
I have something to admit.

Part Two:

Looking at all the girls and still called (for you) dibs

Yes, yes, yes. I admit that I am such a kid

All of my feeling for you...

It honestly feels like some kind of rush

Acting like a kid, you've still get me to blush

On my life, you are my heart's crush

Telling the world that I loved you (Yes, I did)

Going into timeout and doing my ten minute bid

Then paying off my friend to let me go for a quid

Then asking him to do a favor for me for a quid

Including upgrading my clothes of style

Giving you a whole new reason to smile

So we can still stand as that power couple

Acting like kids, we can be that young couple

Standing tall and running the whole playground

Laughing hard until time starts to slow down

You and me saying dreams that can be achievable

All my words and actions will stand as unbeatable

When we make each other feel carefree and fearless

Doing something new with levels of creativity

You in my life have all kinds of positivity

Kissing you still gives me electricity

Time for me to continue in this activity

Part Three:

At snack time, this is what I will write down

That we should get married at the playground

You giggled yes as my friends yelled touchdown!

Bringing in the winds and some rain clouds

Your friends were on one side of the slide

My friends were on the other side of the slide

Puffed up lips and we shared our first kiss
Up and down we started jumping
Holding hands like it was nothing
I always feel better after we finish hugging
If you and I should ever break up,
Yes, I will pout for some weekends
Guess one day, I will have to grow up
One day you will return to my route as friends
Just hug me from behind when we make-up

#115 Bad at Love (I'm Trying)

Part One:
I've been looking for love in all the wrong places
On the days where I'm simply typing,
I've been looking for love in all the wrong races
On the nights where I'm simply swiping,
Betting on love, but no answer from above
I've been doing this shit all wrong
It's just for the purpose of this song
Writing a new tune and she calls it fiction
Singing a new tune and she won't listen
Buying too many flowers and candy
Gifts are not something to do liberally
Giving my love out so generously
Darcy warned me so dangerously
Overcomplimenting like I'm reciting a spell
Smiled, you stood up and said later Maxwell

Bridge:
Realizing that she wasn't meant to be mine,
I go out in the night to find another dime
Hoping that I don't do the same old line
Tried to change, but I couldn't fix my crime

Chorus:
Call this wrong timing, but I'm simply
Bad at love, bad at love, bad at love
Call this wrong timing, but I'm simply
Bad at love, bad at love, bad at love
Call this wrong timing, but I'm simply

Singing, Writing, Climbing, Rhyming
Trying to duel away with the mistakes

Part Two:
Next girl came and I swore she was going to be forever
We created more pain than some pleasure
Turning sunny into rainy type of weather
Texting only, our love became lesser and lesser
Turning our relationship into two fighting monsters
Opposites attract right? Who the hell told that spite?
You did woman; but I think that it will get better
Sarcasm vibes when I'm feeling under pressure
Light up our last fight like a projector
Shine my faults and I'll find a successor

Bridge:
Realizing that she wasn't meant to be mine,
I go out in the night to find another dime
Hoping that I don't do the same old line
Tried to change, but I couldn't fix my crime

Chorus:
Call this wrong timing, but I'm simply
Bad at love, bad at love, bad at love
Call this wrong timing, but I'm simply
Bad at love, bad at love, bad at love
Call this wrong timing, but I'm simply
Singing, Writing, Climbing, Rhyming
Trying to duel away with the mistakes

#116 A Million Poems... (Won't Save You)

I see it (written) all so far,

> but it won't get me (smitten) very far

No matter how many words you scribe

No matter how many words….

No matter how many…

One, Ten, Twenty, Fifty, One hundred or even….

A million poems…

> Won't save you…

Actions will.

So, where the hell are your actions?

Seriously, screw your intentions & infatuations

Seriously, screw your intentions & seductions

Seriously, screw your intentions & dalliances

Seriously, screw your intentions & devotion

Stop praising her body and her sexuality

Why don't you write about her personality?

Why are you echoing what she already knows?

You really believe your words makes her glow?

They will eventually fade like a shadow in the sun

Skillfully, this is how you tell women that they are the one?

God, I sincerely hope that they all truly like hell they run

No matter how many words you scribe

No matter how many words…

No matter how many…

One, Ten, Twenty, Fifty, One hundred or even…

A million poems…

> Won't save you

Actions will.

So, where the hell are your actions?

#117 (Her) Finest (Hour)

Part One:
Welcome the ones who are bold to compete in this competition
Raise your hands as the crowd shower you in pure adoration
Need you so badly, I skipped a Declaration of Introduction
(Pause)
Riding in my Phantom, you're calling me on my phone
Salaciously saying, I can't wait for us to be truly alone
My hearts at a ransom, I'm speeding towards your home
Opened the door and I almost dropped to the floor
That Slyness flare, that Lioness hair
Pretty blue bra and panties set
Those matching lipstick and stocking
The whole world needs to stop talking
My mind is racing for her ignition
Tonight, let's not summon the sun
Three Kisses
                    to calm
                        (down)
                                this one…
She said just to keep calm and listen
As I make you really smitten for me

Part Two:

How do I even start this?

In eyes in the beholder

I see you as a pure goddess

Agreeing with the angel on my shoulder

I want you at your hottest

When you come out of the kitchen

Exotic; you're full of sweet ambition

Covered in cake called Chantilly

Berries and Cream Provocatively

Can you please tell me...?

How to love you amorously?

Dead to Rights, this is your motive

Wheels churning deep on this bass

Time's racing fast like a locomotive

Don't want to lose you in this chase

You always look so amazing in lace

I want you and so much more

You smiled; that's fine

Take me straight to the floor

In your style, we've got time

Then we can have an encore

Just bring us some red wine

Part Three:

Besides making that come true

Look at what you made me do,

I sing about you like chantey

The siren songs of manipulation

When you wear those panties

Perfect, perfect harmonization

You're supporting my individually

I'm supporting your personality
Credibility in your remarkable versatility
and Unspeakable flexibility
Recklessly Speaking, you give me that heated simplicity
All you want is to be deeply appreciated
So long as we ride through this tour together
I promise to come through in all your adventures

#118 Elusive

The Declaration of Introduction:
When this world tries to make us frantic
You by my side, let's knuckle up
Your touch is as equal as being tantric
You by my side, let's double up
Any type of love from you is romantic
Back to the bed, let's cuddle up
(She's) Ready, (I'm) Set, (Let's) Go!

Part One:
This night is worth the state of fascination
We're two stepping in your bedroom when our song comes on
Enjoying each other's company with no type of distraction
You have a cup in your hand as we laugh and dance on
Recklessly Speaking, I'm liking what I am seeing
Moving closer to you and you're inviting me in
Hands around your waist as we move to the rhythm
Grinding slow to get in the mood quickly
I'm feeling you and you're feeling me
Let's move into this moment casually
Our clothes disappearing rapidly
You're with this type of strategy
Let's move to the bed and stare in the galaxy
All the oceans and the stars on your ceiling
But we don't have to move that far
Let's exchange words that's too revealing
I'm your obsession when I ease your tension

Part Two:

In the darkest skies, lightning strikes when we think naughty

When we are close, we will feel the sparks in our bodies

In this room with champagne and glowing neon lights

Round of applause as we both go Beyond the Night

The best case of Acceleration to reach that destination

Tonight I want you and me to chill

Easing our mind on some Turkish tea

No sex, just us feeling this thrill

Love you down and work with me

Your body on my body on this easy dub

Like we are in an underground R&B club

Where it's you, me, and the sound of music

Blend into the night, let's become elusive

#119 (2 Shots of) Sex & Photography

The Declaration of Double Introduction:
Pose with me in this art of photography
Wear that sports bra set in burgundy
Move to the beat of choreography
Fast or slow, Show me your spirituality
Time-lapse; going cosmically
My Five Suns of Amatory
Return here for our photography
Shall we jump into this imagery?
(She's) Ready, (I'm) Set, (Let's) Go!

Part One & Two:
On the seashore of the melatonin
Body shaped with those pretty nipples
As my eyes simply do some roaming
I'm more impressed with your dimples
That's pretty good line for an opening
Recklessly, I come to you once more in the dead of night
Something like a baseline confession
One kiss to your cheeks to make them red with delight
Something like this baseline seduction
Over a picnic under the stars with conversation
Color Me Badd, But I Wanna Sex You Up
Playing old song vibes, but that's what's up
In all my sonnets, least I'm being honest
Sharing what I mastered is significant
Smooth surface now laced with ripples
That's the outline of your panties

(Take Two)

Take this camera and let's take some body shots

Of you and all your poses

Then shower you with roses

Reading your body language

Sexy in the style of savagery

Focusing on all your positions

Pressing down on the shutter button

There I'll say you are legendary

Now I'm staring into the camera lens

You are such a beautiful image

Taking two shots let's do it again

I don't want this night to finish

#120 Memories

Rubber Duckies,

    Campfires in the middle of nowhere,

        Cornballs and solo cups,

            Pineapples & Wally World,

                Finest Jewelry,

            Boss Lady Vibes,

        Expensive red wine on a cool summer evening,

    Lessons of loving yourself,

"cherished, loved, respected, and worthy, not to mention spoiled…"

    Vodka Shot Saturdays & Taco Tuesdays,

        Wine O'Clock,

        Pop Songs,

            Country Songs,

        A long Love Song that I never get tired of listening to,

        Playful love like teenagers,

Kissing in the rain, cuddling to relieve the pain,

    Double Shot of Pineapples,

        Quicks and Perks,

        Manhattan's Fool's Gold

           Second Piece of my Heart,

                Travelling Buddies

Blackberry Cîroc & Lemonade

            Home Cooked Meals,

    Watching game shows at 22:00,

    Dancing & Cooking with passion

        Nighttime walks in Downtown Chicago,

        Game Night

            (2) Date Night

A never-ending debate of Pancakes versus Waffles

Dalliances   vs.   Devotion

Normal is Overrated

You Remind Me of...

Memories of Dalliances and Devotion

I'm often known to speaking in codes,

Mixing the truth and some fantasies

Down this life filled with bumpy roads

Moments where I did and didn't blow it

At the end of all these testimonies

Hoping that you will see right through it…

By the end of this session, you will understand it all.

When you read this and see which one of us will fall.

Who are you going to believe at the end of this story?

It's time to tell you the Entire Truth…

Welcome to The Five Suns of Amatory V:

Memories of Dalliances and *Devotion*

#121 Right This Wrong (Scratch That)

Part One:
We all have our doubts every now and then
But remember that I always have a plan
From companionship to relationships
No communication and my fears take over
Thinking that you and I are over
You're dating again while I'm simply praying again
But I don't know what I am dealing (with)
I'm fighting all the feelings (shit)
Including repeating all my words like a parrot
Including me buying you the biggest karat
All the times we spent together should merit
I need you to either choose me
Or say goodbye and lose me

Pre-Chorus:
Tell me if you still want me as your man
(I'm not accepting simply being your friend)
Tell me if you still want me as your man
(I'm not accepting simply being your friend)

Chorus:
Maybe I should let her go?
(Scratch that)
Will she say yes or no?
(Scratch that)
These feelings, I can't avoid
(Scratch that)

No, I'm not going paranoid
(Scratch that)
Everything we've been through, don't let that be destroyed
I know that you won't wait this long
So, It's time to right this wrong

Part Two:
I'm not a man that's used to begging
But now I'm looking up at Heaven
And this is what I am telling
Please don't write her out of my life
I know that she has the acrimonious choice
In the end, I will not cause no strife
When she walks away from me with no voice
Let's go into my nightmare…again
I'm lost in my mind with no answer
No response or notice from my cell
I'm lost in my mind with no answer
I'm falling back into my personal hell
I'm competing with demons that want you as a snack
I'm representing you when I write about you on tracks
I'll do anything to win you and your whole heart back

Pre-chorus:
Tell me if you still want me as your man
(I'm not accepting simply being your friend)
Tell me if you still want me as your man
(I'm not accepting simply being your friend)

Part Three:

I need you to believe me
I always have a plan
Babe, please don't leave me
Say that I'm still your man
You're my reason to breathe
Don't bury me underneath
All those men after your heart
Please don't give them a start
They may look good by appearance
Please don't give them your clearance
All I need is time and perseverance
Remember that we work together
I want you to be my love forever

Chorus:

Maybe I should let her go?
(Scratch that)
Will she say yes or no?
(Scratch that)
These feelings, I can't avoid
(Scratch that)
No, I'm not going paranoid
(Scratch that)
Everything we've been through, don't let that be destroyed
I know that you won't wait this long
So, It's time to right this wrong

#122 Ten Reasons to Live

The Declaration of Introduction:
Nightlives after Nightlives
Days are skipped completely
In my cup of sweet whisky
Altered by visions and promises of the past and future
Faulty prescription prescribed with numerous decision
Ready and willing to fight reality towards this collision
Recklessly Typing, but what do I want in this life?
The bathtub is running as the steam starts to consume the room
You poured my favorite soap down as it consumes the room
Washing away the world and the uncertainties
Just whisper to my ears and tell me that I'm not dead
Tell me that I am much more than my adversaries
With your voice of understanding, this is what she said

**Part One, Two, Three, Four, Five, Six,
Seven, Eight, Nine & Ten:**
I know that you want to become an *Author*
Maybe become the *Pirate* that rules the waters
Then tell the exciting tale when you're a *Father*
Fly in the skies like a *Pilot*
In the skies when it's quiet
I know that you will like it
Position yourself as a *Musician*
Where the people will want to listen
I know that you have the ambition
Be a *Poet* and let the world know it
Lyrically, you have the skills to show it
Full respect if you want to be an *Architect*
Sculpting from marble to emulating a leader

Ruler of the sands called the Sphinx
Become a *Mixologist* making drinks
All making me money to buy minks
The roars of laugher ignite a *Comedian*
In this life, we are all playing Medium
Become a *Game Show Host* for the ages
Bringing excitement to all standing as a Gladiator
It won't feel like you are doing it for the wages.
Whatever you decide, I'll be your motivator
No matter what you choose in any profession
Let nothing stop you towards those connections

#123 Yaas Queen

Part One:
Girl, I'm feeling myself, feeling myself
Shouts out to the OG Queen B
Making money, I need another shelf
Of all my awards, such a reward
Basic bitches better get on board
Don't listen to those rumors
Those other wannabes bring me humor
But I got a man that's such a crooner
Still living like we're honeymooners
Loving when he makes me special
Rock and roll to some heavy metal
When he covers me in rose petals
I'm confident, relevant, extravagant
Yet my haters call me arrogant
No wonder they are irrelevant

Chorus:
So, I'm bopping to the right to say
Yaas (Queen) Yaas (Queen) Yaas (Queen) Yaas (Queen)
So, I'm bopping to the left to say
Yaas (Queen) Yaas (Queen) Yaas (Queen) Yaas (Queen)
Raise your hands up and say…
This queen got moves sharper than a dagger
This queen got skills with some swagger
I'm all in your mind, that's what matters
Raise your hands up and say…
Yaass (Queen) Yaas (Queen) Yaas (Queen) Yaas (Queen)

Part Two:

From one Queen to another Queen

Call me by name of who I am (daily)

Shining better than a star on a movie screen

Even Janet Jackson said Dammn Baby

From the way I talk and the way I walk

So starstruck, you girls are out of luck

From the way I roll like an armored truck

I'm such a boss, they all call me a rich chick

Woman to Woman, let me hear your pitch quick

Girl, I'm laughing harder than Dolomite

No time to entertain the prototypes

Riding better than a motorbike

I'm the queen that's the hype

Lyrics so fly, I'll have your man turned inside out

No shame as I do this recklessly when I slide out

Me and my girls, this is how we gonna ride out

Chorus:

So, I'm bopping to the right to say

Yaas (Queen) Yaas (Queen) Yaas (Queen) Yaas (Queen)

So, I'm bopping to the left to say

Yaas (Queen) Yaas (Queen) Yaas (Queen) Yaas (Queen)

Raise your hands up and say…

This queen got moves sharper than a dagger

This queen got skills with some swagger

I'm all in your mind, that's what matters

Raise your hands up and say…

Yaas (Queen) Yaas (Queen) Yaas (Queen) Yaas (Queen)

#124 World Peace

The Declaration of Introduction:
You are a gift from the Maker
I would become your builder
Walk around to see your pillars
I would give you the world if you ask for me
A breath of fresh air when you pass me
You are the *Second Piece of My Heart*
Even when Father Time placed us apart
I still return for you to take my name
No one can ever take your part
Literally, life to me is such a game
Now, you go on and press start
(She's) Ready, (I'm) Set, (Let's) Go!

Part One:
I used to look up at the sky
When life made me feel lonely
And really tried not to cry
Sighed at love and said if only
Hearts been broken many times
Continuously scripting so many lines
Waring at feeling of rejections
Yearning for some confirmation
Where hate is not the only view
God, is it possible for one clue?
Of something that is peaceful
For my life to have a sequel
Then he smiled and brought me you
And said she is your equal

Part Two:
You and me, I love it that we can coast
All day and all night in this life, let's boast
I said it before, but it is worth the repeat
When the sun is down.
Can we have some fun right now?
On some fancy drinks and silly banter
I can go all night with you
On some curly fries and fancy wine
Classic line. Fast forward to this time
Candlelight under the stars date
Raspberries and lava cakes to elevate
Your smile and your laugh
I'm so addicted to your voice
When you use it for persuasion
When you use it for education
When you use it for seduction
When you go for the conviction
Yes Girl, I want to fit the description
Change your whole life with no regrets
Spin you around and call you the best
So glad that I got that all off my chest

Part Three:

One chance with you and I'll dance

Left, right, left, right,

Waves bouncing back and forth

Left, right, left, right,

Our heartbeat in sync

Grant me just one drink

Pulses makes me think

When shit goes down, we can just go now

Speeding down the road in my Phantom

You're so amazing, nothing random

World Peace girl, this is your anthem

#125 Fight for Me

Part One:
Lord, I don't often stand by your way
With your infinite help and unconditional love
Lord, I don't often pave in your way
With your infinite help and unconditional love
I need your love and your correction
I give you all my attention
Lord, you only stand as perfection
Yes, I take it all for granted
Open my eyes, let me be enchanted
You gladly paid for my life in ransom
So, I won't become a soulless phantom
When my soul feels like floating
I sing to you until I'm soaring

Chorus:
Lord, Lord, Lord
You are willing to fight for me
Lord, Lord, Lord,
You are willing to fight for me
Lord, Lord, Lord,
You are willing to fight for me
Even when I have done wrong
I beg for your forgiveness
It is not your will to see me gone
Second chances; I'm a witness
Glory hallelujah, Glory hallelujah!
That's why I praise you in this song!

Part Two:

Even with a failing spirit,

I will give you my greatest praise

Even when my strength begins to fall

You will restore it all and make me tall

Your people's soul: you will save them all

As I stand with you with a war cry

I know that the battle is yours

I know that the victory is yours

Part Three:

When my time is up

There I will look up

To see you happy to see me

Overcoming my trials and my tribulation

Welcoming me in your courts; such celebration

Overcoming my trials and my tribulation

Welcoming me in your courts; such celebration

Chorus:

Lord, Lord, Lord

You are willing to fight for me

Lord, Lord, Lord,

You are willing to fight for me

Lord, Lord, Lord,

You are willing to fight for me

Even when I have done wrong

I beg for your forgiveness

It is not your will to see me gone

Second chances; I'm a witness

Glory hallelujah, Glory hallelujah!

That's why I praise you in this song!

#126 Last Forty

Part One & Two:
Laying in your bed right into the morning
Didn't leave your place, that's really something
Since I'm not that type of guy to play and stay
Something about your style got me thinking
I spent my last forty on coffee and smokes
I really wished that last line was a joke
Last night between us was one for the books
You took the reign and started this show
We did it all in your place with some intermission
One kiss and then you started to cook
Teased me with your food to get me back in the position
Girl, you really got that slender look
Body up to the counter against the nook
Reaching that climax and then we both got to relax
You wanted to cuddle in our secluded bubble
Conversation wise, going deeper than any type of abyss
Spinning on some records as we go into some bliss
Taking me with you, let's share one more soul kiss

Part Three & Four:
Last night between us was one for the books
Watching cartoons in the living room
You spent your last forty on lingerie and liquor
We can stay in and make some dinner
I can cook up your favorite dish
Warm waffles, bacon, and some berries
Feeling's getting sweeter than cherries

I treat you right if you bring in the night

I eat you right if you say it is alright

All your clothes, I want stripped off

Eyes rolling as I get you licked off

Up in the air is where we linger

One taste of your fingers

Got my raging lust to simmer

We go deeper and deeper in the moment

My beats, your sounds, let's make some music

Trust me love, I'm all yours for this amusement

#127 (The) Freshly Polished Diamond (Letter)

Maybe short term you get to say you're the lucky one, but you coming into my life with all of your love has forever changed me and opened me up to a world I didn't think ever existed therefore I'd say I'm the luckiest person in the world my love.

What you say is true. But I've been waiting to be with someone that would be what I desire. Someone that has given me a reason to laugh harder, smile longer and like me for me. You. You fit the description and I'm so happy that I chose right that night and you chose me too. You mean the world to me.

Babe, you are one in a million and mean the world to me too. Your words make me weak in the knees and having you love me for every goofy, crazy weirdness I have means so much. You make me feel cherished, loved, respected, and worthy, not to mention spoiled and that means more than you will ever know.

All of that you deserve as my girlfriend and the woman in my life that has a special place in my heart right now. As you shine like a freshly polished diamond.

#128 Once in a Lifetime

The Declaration of Introduction:
It took me a while before I slowed down
Looking closely in the mirror
To get it all together before having you around
You're getting clearer
The Grape Vine said to give you a brand-new crown
You're the real winner
Once in a lifetime love babe, I'm forever bound
You're the real winner
(She's) Ready, (I'm) Set, (Let's) Go

Part One:
Picture this…
Rocking new clothes and that fresh fade,
While cruising behind these shades
Picture this…
Drinking Berry Cîroc in my lemonade,
Recklessly publishing my serenades
Doing what I love and still getting paid
Riding wild like a Reckless Renegade
While obtaining all my True Luxuries
I swear I'm living this life in harmony
Soaring up there on sky street
Girl you are such a fly beat
You're my Heaven and Reality
Bridging everything to complete

Part Two:

By day and by night,

Aren't you a breath of fresh air?

By day and by night,

With those styles in your hair?

You make a move and we all stare

Step against you, who would even dare?

Vibes of the First Lady, salutes to you my baby

So fresh and so elegant

Let's call you heaven sent

You can be that queen in those magazines

Cover of Essence, they'll know your presence

Pictured in Vogue, let's go full rogue

Going into la la land, let's dream on

While I keep writing your theme song

Playing the Keys, being Unbreakable

You're my piano ballad

Playing the Keys, doing the Unthinkable

All my actions are valid

Writing for security and stability

Fighting for security and stability

Singing for security and stability

Bringing you security and stability

It's worth spending all that energy

People often had to stop and stare

Power couple vibes, what a pair

One of kind love we have so rare

Fitting together like a puzzle

Silencing our haters with muzzles

We're turning into that power couple
Who buys everything on the double
Sipping drinks with the bubbles
Running this life with no trouble
When our enemies simply crumble

#129 Lay It Down

Part One:
Going for your heart was the aim
Deep down, I bet that you feel the same
You and me, let's start with our names
As humans, what do we have to proclaim?
Searching for something substantial
All types of love even interracial
We found each other; it's potential
The whole world isn't getting easier
The whole world is getting greedier
Lazy love is making me sleepier
I want love to feel like a meteor
Burning through my atmosphere
That warm flash covered in stars
Reappearing like a chandelier
As we dance in the ballroom
The dark ceiling needing some color
As we dance in the bedroom
So, our universe won't get any duller
Look at what we can do with each other
Dropping bath bombs revealing the prize
An oasis of a beautiful vision of us
Stellar Collusion reveals our cosmic eyes
Hand in hand, let's go create some trust

Part Two:

Going for my heart was your aim
Perfect shot as it goes in flame
One touch and you feel the same
The warmth and beating for you
Like the sound of rhythm and blues
So in tune, let's listen to a throwback
My feelings for you, not gonna hold back
All this adoration, give me some feedback
When life wants to bring in detours
Be my shield, I'll be your sword
I'll work hard until you feel secure
We go together like one accord
Loving you deeply is such a reward
So let's build so then we can chill
Up in a mansion right up the hill
Let's be each other's piece of mind
Disregarding the meaning of time
Serenading the meaning of my lines
I give you loyalty, you call me Royalty
I give you my crown to profess it all
Break your walls and watch it fall
Decompress all our stress
Come and rest on my chest
Hold each other at full length
Use each other for full strength
Go out and create new adventures
You and me in so many pictures
Right there I can see our future

#130 Will you be My... (#33 Remix)

The Declaration of Introduction:
Somewhere I was going to write a part two
But these words still reign true
I'll give you my all to the very last cent
Because for you, it would be *Love Well Spent*
Hope you like these brand-new confirmations
I go back to remember the reasons why I wanted you in my life
(She's) getting ready for my question, (I'm) about to make her
an Honest Woman, (Let's) Go

Part One: Best (Girl) Friend:
Do you remember how we first met?
When I first complimented your personality?
You didn't even give me your name yet
But I couldn't let you get away that easily
There was something about your spirit
Heaven and Reality, yes you read it
Asked for your name as I gave you mine
In my mind, I called you a perfect dime
We walked into that famous coffee shop
Took a picture together, didn't need Photoshop
Felt like hours as we talked about who we were
Hopes and dreams to what made us happy
This wasn't even a date, but it felt like fate
That day turned out nicely
We exchanged numbers to stay in touch
Days turned to months, seeing each other regularly
At the coffee shop in the morning and the evening

One night I knew I was going to ask you eventually
To be my Best (Girl) Friend
And here we are ever since then

Part Two: Girlfriend

Do you remember when you wanted me as your boyfriend?
We were still being best friends and I didn't get the signs
When you dressed up for me and I didn't even notice
Giving me flirty compliments and I didn't even notice
Brought my other friend with me and you got jealous
Old souls told me "what were you thinking?" (tell us)
When you got closer than we did at that restaurant?
Time and wine made our moment so nonchalant
The other guest saw us as a couple
I just smiled and that's where I stumbled
Yes, when other guys were hollering for your attention
Hate to say it, but I became jealous for your attention
Eros did that as a warning that you would not wait forever
Do you remember when I wanted you as my girlfriend?
When I stopped being so reckless against my feelings
Your beauty, brains and style finally got me thinking
Maybe you and me should be exclusive
You'll be my woman and I'll be your man
Remember that I will always have a plan
Home cooked all your favorite meals in the basket
Made it a night to remember as I took out a gift
You smiled and quickly opened the gift
That diamond key necklace you saw by the coffee shop.
You gave me a hug and gave me my first kiss with you.
I told you that I liked you and then you said the same
Quickly, I asked you if you would be my girlfriend
And here we are even since then

Part Three: Fiancée

Staying in a relationship longer than my last one
Shamelessly, all those girls were just past fun
You made me a better man every time we are together
So little time in this life, I want you to be my forever
On the same vibe of love, sex or whatever
You can still have all my endeavors
I'm taking a chance for you to be my whole world
On everything, I just want you to be my only girl
I will get down on one knee right away
Preparing my voice with a firm tone
And ask you proudly to be my Fiancée
Give you this ring with your birth stone
You squealed yes and laughed finally!
I would choose you all over again
And here we are ever since then

Part Four: Wife

I've said it before, and I will say these parts again
Anything you want, I'll spend it to the last cent
Anything for you will still be Love Well Spent
God, I'm about to marry my best (girl) friend!
Fresh cut fade with a black suit and tie
White dress with sparkles around you with an angelic glow
Time to continue and clarify
You still are the true Miss London Star of this wedding show!
I can no longer imagine you without my life
So here we are about be husband and wife
As we finally stand here with families and friends
Hand in hand, here we are ever since then.

#131 My (Sanctioned) Actions (Poetic Interlude)

The Declaration of Intro-lude:

For your love, I would go to such strength

For your trust, that would give me strength

Sounds so poetic, but it's starting to feel pathetic

Words can only go so far before they start to fade

As I become to go into the realm of a Renegade

Where this villain is emulated as the heroic

Listen to me as I recklessly make this poetic

They say that love is crime,

Yes, I'm down to do the time

Where most guys wouldn't even start to

Doing things that I thought I would never do

Roaming and shopping on Fifth Avenue

Buying you diamonds for the snow season

Flying straight to the islands for no reason

I'm travelling back and forth like tennis

Any place you want, including Paris

Pay a year's rent then we go to Venice

When it comes to shopping, it's for sensual pleasure

The clothes, the shoes, and the expensive lingerie

Basically, I'm calling you the new national treasure

Taking all responsibilities; I did all of this for you

My poetic words will be sanctioned as ammunition

No games, but this level is getting a bit hard

Learning how to maneuver around your guards

From my actions moonlighting as Seduction
Securing your heart without getting iced or charred
Truthfully speaking, you just want some recognition
Guess I should have start off with this introduction
But I'm better off writing this as an intermission

#132 That (Whimsical, but Illustrious) Finale: Pluviophile

Part One, Two, Three:
Read closely towards this vision
Your aroma infused in this rhythm
Elegantly Burning
Attractively glowing
Smoke escalating graciously
Your body moves charmingly
Serenading on a boundless range
As you sing on this commotion
The music begins to change…
Playing skillfully on this floor
Moving tastefully in slow motion
Shall we commence on this tour?
My mind is in a dark, but sultry place
Stand proudly as I continue this fiery illusion
You are that flirting spirit in your primal heat
Curves of multicolor fires; amazement for the ages
On some deep sexual healing that's worth kneeling
Where the bass is deep and the tempo is low
When it comes to the weather, I'm a Pluviophile
When it come to the weather, I'm a Ceraunophile
When we are together, Let's become Clinophile
Drinking all kinds of wine, acting like Oenophiles
Background sounds are playing in reverse
Stars in our eyes, welcome to our universe
We're in so deep I'm in your Nebulous Skies
Pupils' dilating, bring out the venomous eyes

Smile is grinning, bring out the feminine alibi
She got me going so low, I'm on my knees
Our shady thoughts that desire to please
Not of words, but of body language mate
A woman of so many talents
The way she's undresses to her eight
She says let's make this happen
On this slow-burning song track
Writing all this line by line
Making this night a comeback
I am yours and you are mine

#133 Penalty

Part One:
I wish that this was all in my head
But here we are instead
Everywhere I look isn't getting clear
In your eyes, I can see a cold world
I didn't think we would ever get here
All those lies, you're getting cold girl
All the times that you stopped smiling
Only hearing the words he's always lying
Truthfully speaking, I'm slowly dying
On the account of claims prefabricated
Leaving me feeling so intimidated
While you stand so infuriated
Got me sickening and questioning
By the end of this, who will stand humiliated?
This relationship is getting so incarcerated
To the point we both cry out to be emancipated

Chorus:
I'm paying for the penalty
And it's messing me up mentally
I'm paying for the penalty
And it's messing me up mentally
I'm paying for the penalty
And it's messing me up mentally

Part Two:

I wish that this was all in my head

But here we are instead

Why do you feel like I took you for granted?

Did I not make your life feel so enchanted?

I had you woven into my life plan

But I guess you rather stand alone

I was ready to stand tall as your man

Guess you don't need me or my Corazon

Now you laugh and said our love be damned

For all the times when my love was draining you

To the point that they had to call in a doctor

I looked into your eyes, you were changing too

You were becoming that sinister type monster

To make the matters worse, it started raining too

Turning our world into a natural disaster

By the end, all that is really remaining is

Chorus:

I'm paying for the penalty

And it's messing me up mentally

I'm paying for the penalty

And it's messing me up mentally

I'm paying for the penalty

And it's messing me up mentally

#134 Perfect Night for Two

Part One:
Here I go again on this segment
Stuck in the past and the present
Makes no sense? Don't get so tense
Staring out in the city from my balcony
A bottle of my favorite drink by me
On the seventh floor with no company
Going in and out of my memory (focus)
When I'm in my feelings for something
The city lights are so bright tonight
Pull out my black shades for show
I need a woman with me, a classy beau
Requesting for a night with you only
Your company is all I require for satisfaction (with some foreplay)
Just desiring some honest conversation (along the way)
You replied accepting my invitation (texting you're on the way)

Part Two:
When you arrived at my place,
Two gentle kisses on your face
Come outside to the balcony
Take some pictures for memories
Even simple talk of yesteryear
I'm so glad that you are here
The volume of the city is turned down
Ushering in two bottles as you bring in the cups with the stem
I'll pour us the first cup to calm the mayhem
Two glasses in and then I call you a gem

Words just to blow off some steam
Maybe it's your slim black jeans
Smiled, you liked to be flattered
Another bottle in and we're getting vulnerable
Recklessly Balanced, but part three is incredible

Part Three:
On some real talk,
All doubts are shattered tonight
Unshackle our thought and emotions
To believing we can go to achievable heights
Unshackle our thought and emotions
Let's lay our demons down for the last time
Zero judgement passed on us
This moment in time with you is liberating
Closing the chasms between us
Let's make it sensual and intoxicating
You on top of me for a minute
Embracing the flush of the wine
It might be worth us going in it
Should we even cross the line?
You kindly said not this time
Citing we should stay on this vibe
Releasing sparks from our talks
On this balcony of just me and you
Make this the Perfect Night for two

#135 The (Warning) Shot

The (Chained) Declaration of Introduction:

Come one, Come all!

Place your bets right here!

Come one, Come all!

Press your luck right here!

Come one everyone,

Take the risk right here!

Come close to the cage…

This is one for the pages

Come close to the cage…

One Heart in chains and one broke free…

To find another…

(She's) Not Here, (I'm) Wondering Why I'm here, (Let's) Go?

Part One:

Remember when I used to make you laugh?

Remember when I used to make you smile?

Remember when I used to make you dance?

Be that guy you called first whenever you got good news?

Now I guess all those things aren't coming true

You were waiting and waiting for me to return

But you stopped holding on for me

This is such a fucked up break up

Why are you making me pay the Penalty?

To the point of me losing my identity?

You're bailing out on keeping us together?

I guess nothing really does last forever

All the photos we took in the past

Oh, how the memory is fading fast
Once our love was such a magic act
Where every day was always a wonder
Now it's become such a tragic act
As you went out to find a new lover

Part Two:
Remember when I was always on your mind?
Remember when I wanted to take all your time?
Remember when I wrote about you in my Rhymes?
You're the only girl that made me feel so alive
But you made me love you like it was a nine to five
Worked harder than before to not bring you heartache
Hoping, wishing, and then praying that we were still okay
Guess you didn't feel it when you said why should I stay?
Filled with so much doubt, guess you did more than pout
Giving me the warning shot when you (made it to this track)
Firing me the warning shot until you (faded into the black)
Played the silence card and got your results
Wanting to be out and made me become single
When I never left you to go out and mingle
Guess you left me with no choice
Woman, where was your voice?

Outro:
Leaving me out in the cold
You really are so bold
Leaving me out in the cold
You really are so... (sigh)
Never mind girl... I fold

#136 That (Whimsical, but Illustrious) Finale II: Opacarophile

Part One:

In this sunset, I'll come correct
As you start this show (now)
Playing on this type of roulette
You know how to glow (wow)
You made yourself very clear
I'm breaking out in cold sweat
A one-way ticket out of here
I'll lay back in my chair and admire
Bringing this moment even higher
When you wear that mini skirt
Teasing me with your mini flirts
Serenading in the style of cajole
Yes, you're in full control
On my mind, body, and soul
Creating a flood of electricity in my body
Pulse rapidly going when we touch instantly
Your skills tonight stand out brilliantly

Part Two:

In this sunset, I'll come correct
As you start this show (now)
Playing on this type of roulette
You know how to glow (wow)
Every time we hung out,
All of you, I want to kiss it
Feeling lusty, you said prove it

Recklessly bringing my tongue out
Riding me well, you're so explicit
Physically, you got me so strung out
Your presences got me so restless
Your beauty makes me breathless
My tongue only speaks Reckless
Kissing you always feels endless

Part Three:
On this lifeline and lifetime on your throne
Where self-love is for your pleasure
Can you imagine the pleasures in your moan?
Still calling you my national treasure
Sipping wine got us hooked on this line
Just one more round for good measure
Sipping wine got us hooked on this line
Leaving time for you is by my design
Staring with serenading before penetrating
Body, mind and soul, time for an upgrading
A gentleman is where I stand, give me some credit
Whatever you want in this life I'll promise to get it
All these words and action, remember who said it

#137 We Ran Out Of Time

The Final Declaration of Introduction:
Even though I will never be called out in cheating,
She calls me out on not being on her side in leaving
Swearing that I would return, she stopped believing
Left me for somebody else, yes, I did some weeping
I'm out of moves of keeping her heart (how defeating)
My heart and mind built my walls up and went to have a meeting
Saying one day you guys will be on good terms worth speaking?
But for now, work on yourself for the better and start your healing.
When you return, maybe then she will start believing in you again...
(She's) Reading, (I'm) Truth Telling, (Let's) Finish this

Part One:
I guess you can say that I'm tripping around
Easing the pain by sipping around
Go round after round
Black out moments of me losing my control
Summoning chaos against your heart and soul
Revealing things that might scare
Being that Monster of a heartbreaker
When the dust settled of this nightmare
Being that Money Robber like the Rainmaker
It is worth writing to steal your heart again?

Part Two:

Well, it hurts my heart that she was the one to be leaving

She begins to laugh and reveal petrifying memories

All my faults and my secrets to my family and friends

That was her way of saying our relationship will end

Worse part, she walks away with a brand-new boyfriend

And I lost her forever as my girlfriend.

Rolled the Vegas dice for the last time…

Guess it's time for me to become that prisoner

Changing actions and words to sound so sinister

I used to love music, now it all sounds so stupid

Talking about love, I'm getting sick to death

Too far. I should stop and take a breath

Connecting new songs to you, that isn't fair

Lost in the lyrics, but my heart couldn't bear

You and him? It's not even worth a stare

New clothes and smile only mask the pain

But I don't want to go completely insane

It's not you that is really driving this mind

Part Three:

We've been through so much

Then we lost touch

We've been through so much

Then we lost touch

Hope you still call me your friend

Even after the pain of you resides

Because I will until this life ends

Later in life, hope you're by my side

Until then…

You and I ran out of time.

#138 We Are Okay

(The) Declaration of Introduction (Finale):
The chorus of Busta Rhymes' song *Decision* is worth the listen
Yes, I want you back as my friend until my end
Even after our time of bitter separation
It gave way for a time of self-appreciation
Recklessly, (I didn't make it) elimination
Last time I'm going on that examination
Even after our time of utter separation
It gave me some time for self-appreciation
Amorously, (in the end) I still find gratification
My love I remembered you in celebration
                    (Final Pause)
It was amazing how God made you
Until one day He said she will trade you
Yes, that line was true to save her pain
So she wouldn't go internally insane
Life lessons needed to learn in order for her to gain maturity
Bring her someone else? (Shit. Fine) No one should be lonely?
But fuck that ruling; I'm breaking out of this book (Security!)
So in the end, I won't go mentally insane
Realizing that loving her won't be the same
Romantically written, this is my final claim
(She's) Ready to listen, (I'm) Set to tell the entire Truth, (Let's) Go and
Really Finish this.

Part Three:

I know that you have been through it all

Times where you have let your walls fall

Then brought it back with guards on call

I've been through the same pain

That's the best part of being human

I've cried until it looked like rain

That's the best part of being human

Even when broken, we still try to be open

Even after you made the acrimonious decision

Dating around, but love was nowhere to be found

One day you plan to read this after our bitter tension

Where I stand in your life… that is my final question

Let me stop there and finally turn this all round

Part Two:

I never was trying to play the hero

But I *know* that I am better than those zeros

Recklessly realizing you are the one from the intro

I listen to all your preferences

What you like and dislike and becoming your melody

Calling me up whenever you wanted some company

My words will stand as evidence

My actions in the same sentence

Of giving what you need here

Let me make myself crystal clear

I want to love you in a special way

When no man had their place to stay

Basically, all night and all day

By the end, tell me that we are okay

(Pause)

470

You don't want a man that'll hesitate
But be with you and give it to you straight
Keep focus on you whenever I concentrate
Easing the burning lust of my selfishness
Crystalizing to the point of hardness
Until it forms into a diamond from my tenderness
Putting it on your finger to show my commitment
Setting this all up for the perfect moment
Staying with me until the end,
You will get a bonus treatment

Part One:
Like sexing twice in the afternoon
Your presence always made me swoon
Chilling and watching some 90's cartoons
I'm a child at heart, you bring it out of me
You accept it from the start and still love me
From all my words and deeds that are not imaginary
You're my whole world in my tales of Amatory
Spelling it all to you in codes of my Vocabulary
Thank you for reading my Five Suns of Amatory

Fin

THE FIVE SUNS OF AMATORY

Playlist

*These are the song references that are paired
to the respective stories in this novel.*

Track One:
The First Declaration of Dedication:
The Infatuation of Satin and Soul

- ♦ #2 *No Air* by Jordin Spark feat. Chris Brown
- ♦ #7 *You Rock My World* by Michael Jackson
- ♦ #7 *Why You Wanna* by T.I
- ♦ #13 *House Party* by Mya
- ♦ #13 *Fallen* by Mya
- ♦ #13 *My Love is Like…Wo* by Mya
- ♦ #13 *Get Right* by Jennifer Lopez
- ♦ #13 *Over the Floor* by Jennifer Lopez (feat. Pitbull)
- ♦ #13 *Diary* by Alicia Keys
- ♦ #13 *Typewriter* by Alicia Keys
- ♦ #13 *Girl on Fire* by Alicia Keys
- ♦ #13 *Unbreakable* by Alicia Keys
- ♦ #13 *Un-Thinkable (I'm Ready)* by Alicia Keys
- ♦ #13 *I Wanna Be Down* by Brandy
- ♦ #13 *Say Yes* by Floetry
- ♦ #13 *Talk About Our Love* by Brandy
- ♦ #13 *Full Moon* by Brandy
- ♦ #13 *Who is She 2 U?* by Brandy
- ♦ #13 *No Role Modelz* by J. Cole
- ♦ #13 *Age Ain't a Number* by Aliyah

- ◆ #13 *Try Again* by Aliyah
- ◆ #16 *Takeyouthere* by Musiq Soulchild
- ◆ #18 *Sumthin' Sumthin'* by Maxwell
- ◆ #18 *Glamorous* by Fergie
- ◆ #23 *Staying Alive* by Bee Gees
- ◆ #24 *Money Dance* by Rick Ross
- ◆ #25 *Little Too Late* by JoJo
- ◆ #27 *Playing Hard* by Trey Songz
- ◆ #28 *The Light* by Common
- ◆ #29 *Can You Stand the Rain* by New Edition
- ◆ #33 *I Can't Help It* by Michael Jackson
- ◆ #36 *Integrity* by Ne-Yo
- ◆ #37 *101 (Interlude)* by Chris Brown
- ◆ #38 *Don't Stray Away (Interlude)* by Marcus Anderson
- ◆ #38 *Takeyouthere* by Musiq Soulchild
- ◆ #38 *Crazy in Love* by Beyoncé
- ◆ #38 *Cater 2 U* by Beyoncé
- ◆ #38 *Dance 4 U* by Beyoncé
- ◆ #40 *No Doubt* by 702
- ◆ #41 *From Time* by Drake
- ◆ #42 *Don't Leave Me* by Blackstreet
- ◆ #42 *Part Time Lover* by H-Town
- ◆ #43 *Rick James* by Keyshia Cole
- ◆ #45 *Runaway Sex* by The-Dream
- ◆ #45 *Angel in Disguise* by Brandy

Track Two:
The Second Declaration of Dedication:
Moonlight of Seduction (Part One)

❤ #51 *Sexual Healing* by Marvin Gaye

❤ #51 *Sumthin' Sumthin'* by Maxwell

❤ #54 *Claire de Lune* by Claude Debussy

❤ #55 *Dear God* by Hunter Hays

❤ #57 *The Softest Place on Earth* by Xscape

❤ #57 *Your Body is the Business* by Avant

❤ #59 *Recovery* by Justin Bieber

❤ #59 *It Is What It Is* by DJ Aktive (feat. Musiq Soulchild)

❤ #66 *No Diggy* by Blackstreet

❤ #66 *Goals* by A-Lex feat. Musiq Soulchild & the Husel

❤ #68 *Lonely* by Demi Lovato

Track Three:
The Third Declaration of Dedication:
Moonlight of Seduction (Part Two)

♣ #87 *Touch of Love* by Slave

♣ #88 *Ruin the Friendship* by Demi Lovato

♣ #88 *One Woman Man* by John Legend

♣ #95 *Crown Royal* by Jill Scott

♣ #96 *My Weed Chic* by Sunny Bo

♣ #96 *L.A Magic* by Fingazz

♣ #96 *Peaches and Cream* by 112

♣ #96 *Peaches N' Cream* by Snoop Dogg

♣ #97 *Break You Off* by The Roots

Track Four:
The Fourth Declaration of Dedication:
Memories of *Dalliances* and Devotion

♠ #102 *Party & Bullshit* by Notorious B.I.G (Biggie Smalls)

♠ #103 *Can You Believe* by Robin Thicke

♠ #103 *Love After War* by Robin Thicke

♠ #106 *Butta Love* by Next

♠ #109 *Partner for Life* by Diddy (feat. Jamie Foxx)

♠ #110 *Either Way & One More Hour* by Anthony Ramos

♠ #119 *I Wanna Sex You Up* by Color Me Badd

Track Five:
The Fifth and Final Declaration of Dedication:
Memories of Dalliances and *Devotion*

♦ #123 *Dammn Baby* by Janet Jackson

❤ #128 *Unbreakable* by Alicia Keys

♣ #128 *Unthinkable (I'm Ready)* by Alicia Keys

♠ #138 *Decision* by Busta Rhymes